# Remnants

# of

# Crypto-Jews

# Among

# Hispanic  Americans

## Gloria  Golden

**Andrea Alessandra Cabello, Editor**
**University of California, Berkeley**
**&**
Sohaib  Raihan

**Floricanto Press**

**ISBN:0-915745-56-9**
Floricanto Press
650 Castro Street, 120-331
Mountain View, California 94041
(415) 552-1879(702) 995 1410 Fax
**www.floricantopress.com**
info@floricantopress.com

# Remnants

# of

# Crypto-Jews

## Other Titles by Floricanto Press:

*Bring Me More Stories: Tales of the Sephardim.* By Sally Benforado. Floricanto Press ISBN: 0915745674

*Brotherhood of the Light: A Novel of the Crypto-Jews and the Penitentes of New Mexico.* By Ray Michael Baca. Floricanto Press. ISBN: 0915745666

# ABOUT THE AUTHOR

Gloria Golden received a degree from the City College of New York, studied photography at the International Center for Photography in New York, Maine workshops, and Santa Fe workshops.

As an accomplished photographer, she has exhibited in many parts of the United States, published articles and lectured on Jewish rituals practiced by descendants of Jews from the Spanish and Portuguese Inquisitions.

This book reveals, through photographs and oral histories, how descendants of the Sephardim within the Hispanic communities of the American Southwest were able to hold on to remnants of a faith that was forcibly taken away from them.

# Acknowledgments

My deepest gratitude goes to my husband, Barry Golden, for his unwavering support from the beginning to the end of this project. I must thank several people who helped me during the five years I have worked on this book. Thanks to my family, David, Rachel, Jen, Michelle, and Elena, whose encouragement boosted my spirits; to María Apodaca and Kim Delgado for their belief in this book, and to all my friends in New Mexico and El Paso, Texas, who gave so much of themselves.

*In Memory of All Those Who Suffered at the Hands of the Inquisitions in Spain, Portugal, and the New World*

# INTRODUCTION

# Judaism:  In Memory and Spirit

Five hundred years after the Spanish and Portuguese Inquisitions, what remains of Judaism?

The oral histories and photographs of Jews descended from Spain and Portugal (Sephardim) speak of an enduring spirituality within families, five hundred years after the Edict of Expulsion from Spain in 1492 and the forced conversions of Portuguese Jews to Catholicism in 1497.

Present-day *conversos* are familiar with the "Golden Age of Spain," a civilization in the tenth and eleventh centuries, when Jews, Christians, and Moors lived side by side peacefully. They worked together, and sometimes prayed together, living in what seemed to have been the best of times. Could anyone have imagined the radical changes that were to take place just a few hundred years later?  Jews, Christians, and Moors could no longer live together, for Spain was to be united in Christianity.

The year 1391 was of critical importance to the Jews, as riots and forced conversions swept through the country. Distinguished Jews of the period began their conversion to Catholicism.  According to Francisco Cantera Burgos, in his book, *La conversión del célebre talmudista Salomón Levi*, and Luciano Serrano, in his book, *Los conversos Pablo de Santa María y Alfonso de Cartagena*, "The most prominent convert of this period was Solomon Halevi, chief rabbi of Burgos, who around 1389 took the name Pablo de Santa María and at Avignon Antipope Benedict XIII's request returned to

## Gloria Golden

Burgos as bishop, where he engaged in conversionist activities" (qtd. in Gitlitz 5).[1] Considering the events that were about to take place, some Jews were motivated to convert for reasons other than religion. Yitzhak Baer, in his book, *A History of the Jews in Christian Spain*, discusses their motives for conversion, indicating that some converted for their own personal gain, economically or politically. Needless to say, sacrificing their Judaic beliefs afforded them greater opportunities (para. in Gitlitz 6).[2]

Yitzhak Baer chronicles the atrocities which befell the Jews in Spain in the late 1300s. He states, "In June of 1391 rioters swept into the Jewish quarter of Seville, burning, raping, looting, destroying fiscal records, and forcibly converting as many Jews as they could to Catholicism. Within days the prosperous Jewish community of Seville lay in ruins. Within a week or two the same fate had befallen most of the rest of Andalucia's Jews" (qtd. in Gitlitz 7).[3] The killing of Jews and forced conversions in Spain created significant dangers for the Sephardim. According to Luis Suárez Fernándes, in his book, *Judíos españoles en la edad media*, most Jews, when faced with death, decided upon conversion (para. in Gitlitz 7).[4]

Following the expulsion of the Jews from Spain in 1492, Jews were not permitted to remain on Spanish territories. Any Jewish person who chose not to leave, had to convert to Catholicism. Without conversion, their choice was to emigrate or be burned at the stake. Some converted and became full-fledged Christians (*conversos* or New Christians). Others converted and practiced Judaism in secret (crypto-Jews). Nevertheless, many in both groups maintained some Jewish traditions, often without knowing the origin of rituals and practices.

This conversion process, for the most part, was a means of survival rather than a true adoption of Catholicism. Erna Paris confirms, "In the three months that elapsed between edict and expulsion thousands of Jews did convert although a sudden love of Christianity can hardly be thought to have motivated them."[5]

The hardships faced upon leaving Spain were horrific for the Spanish Jews. Paris vividly describes the following: Although some Jews "traveled by donkey," the Jews of Spain, for the most part, walked out of their country. These refugees were the "scholars, the sons and daughters of families who had served their monarchs . . . shoemakers, tanners, butchers, the old, the pregnant, [and] the young."[6] Extraordinary weather conditions, in the heat of summer, and the harshness of the land caused many to endure severe suffering.[7]

The Jews who had so much pride in their achievements could not believe their banishment. How many were able to withstand the numerous obstacles confronting them as they tried to leave Spain? Traveling conditions were quite dangerous, especially in unsafe ships. Yet, many chose exile, and as Paris explains, "Those who chose exile were, for the most part, the salt-of-the-earth of Spanish Jewry: the artisans, the tradesmen, and the women—the historical carriers of religious tradition."[8] An extraordinary civilization was lost in Iberia, probably to never again regain its glory.

Having suffered greatly in their efforts to leave Spain, many Jews returned. As Andrés Bernaldez, in his book, *Memorias del Reinado de los Reyes Católicos*, and L. Suárez Fernández, in *Documentos Acerca de la Expulsión de los Judíos*, explain, "[many were] in rags, barefoot, and full of lice, [and others were] dying of hunger" (qtd. in Paris 251). [9] Suárez Fernández further explains that according to Spanish law, return to Spain meant baptism (para. in Paris 251).[10]

Spanish Jews went to Portugal and many other parts of the world. "Thousands sailed for North Africa, Italy (Pope Alexander asked all the Italian States to receive them), Flanders, the Low Countries, the south of France, and the lands of the expanding Ottoman Empire."[11]

## Gloria Golden

Portugal, because of its proximity to Spain, was a likely destination for many of the exiled Jews. Although they had been there a few years, one could never have imagined what they would have to bear. Now, as Portuguese Jews, they were faced with some of the harshest treatment, as they were at risk of losing their children if they didn't agree to convert. "In 1497, King Manuel of Portugal ordered the forced conversion of all Jews in his country, including those who had arrived just five years earlier at the time of the Spanish Expulsion."[12] As Seymour Liebman explained, the Jews who did not wish to convert were directed to leave Portugal. However, the children were prevented from accompanying their parents, and conversion was to be forced upon them. If, on the other hand, the parents converted, they would be able to keep their children. Most Jews decided upon conversion. These Portuguese inhabitants are referred to as the *anusim* (Heb., forced ones).[13]

"Many *conversos*, in trying to distance themselves from the Holy Office of the Inquisition, immigrated to the New World. This was their hope for a better life, free from persecution. Liebman informs us that the New World was divided by Spain into viceroyalties, which included "New Spain (Mexico)" and "New Castile (Peru)." He explains further that "Mexico consisted of what is now the southwestern United States, all of Mexico and Central America, the Spanish islands in the Caribbean, principally Santo Domingo, Puerto Rico, and Cuba, and, in the Far East, the Philippines."[14]

How did Sephardim reach the New World? "There were at least six Jews with Columbus on his first voyage,"[15] and many came later with *conquistadores*. In *The New World Interlopers: The Portuguese in the Spanish West Indies from Discovery to 1640*, Henry H. Keith has indicated that, "Portuguese Jews often served as sailors on the ships that smuggled Jews into the New World" (qtd. in Liebman 19).[16] Why did they come to Spanish territory? "The Sephardim who came to the New World in the late Middle Ages elected this residence despite the necessity for secrecy and the danger of living in the shadow of the Holy Office of the Inquisition. They preferred to live among those who shared their secular ethnicity."[17] The Jews from Spain felt great pride in being Spanish and came to the New World filled with that same pride. One can still feel the importance given to this heritage through the voices of their descendants today.

Between the years 1493 and 1802, Spain repeatedly "issued decrees" prohibiting Jews and Moors from entering its territories. Liebman believed that the reason for so many decrees was that Jews living in the colonies disregarded them and continued living there without authorization.[18]

The arrival of the Inquisition in the New World changed the lives of the Jews in the colonies. They again had to contend with fear of the Inquisition on their territory and hide their Jewish practices. The tribunals arrived when, according to Richard E. Greenleaf, in his book, *Zumárraga and the Mexican Inquisition*, "In 1569, King Philip II decreed the establishment of tribunals of the Holy Office in Mexico and Peru. Reports had been sent to the king and his father, Charles I (also served as Charles V of the Holy Roman Empire), about Jews swarming into the New World" (qtd. in Liebman 22).[19]

In addition to the arrival of the above tribunals, another "tribunal [was] established in Cartagena on July 25, 1610."[20]

Jews demonstrated a fierce belief system as they clung to the tenets of their faith. They tried their best to hold on and avoid slipping away from Judaism. However, the Inquisition was aware of their practices. Seth Ward explains:

When Spain established the Inquisition in her New-World colonies, inquisitors soon found much evidence of "Judaizing." Whether from loyalty to Judaism or fear of the Inquisition . . . many New Christians found their way to remote areas. Research documentation is particularly strong about New Christian settlement in what later became northern New Mexico and southern Colorado. Inquisition records clearly indicate, however, that throughout the Spanish empire the Holy Office located individuals who expressed loyalty to the "Law of Moses" rather than to Christianity, and suffered the consequences.[21]

Moses, who led the Jews out of Egypt, and Queen Esther, who saved the Jewish people of Persia, "were seen [as a source of salvation for] Jewish people from alien religious oppression."[22] Moses was seen as a savior for leading them towards freedom and giving them their law. The "Law of Moses" speaks of the Israelites receiving their law, given by God, through Moses on Mount Sinai. The Ten Commandments are part of this law. Gitlitz states that, "For most early *conversos* Moses . . . was the traditional Jewish Biblical hero."[23] Present-day *conversos* may not be certain of their Jewish heritage from Spain, but Moses has been mentioned in their homes.

What were the consequences for "Judaizing"? There was great suffering in the New World and always fear that one would be accused of Judaizing and called before the Inquisition. Liebman, in his book, *New World Jewry, 1493-1825: Requiem for the Forgotten*, explains:

> Torture was less frequent than is popularly believed; it never occurred at an early stage of the proceedings, and it was administered only when, after several warnings and opportunities to confess, the prisoner insisted on his innocence, refusing to admit the truth. . . . The most common form of torture in the New World was the *potro*, a bed like frame with straps from side to side upon which the prisoner was placed, naked. The prisoner's limbs were strapped with leather bands, and tightened by the turns of a wheel, causing excruciating pain. Often, a prisoner would confess after the first turn of the wheel. . . . The ultimate penalty was the stake. Two groups of

people qualified for the stake: unrepentant heretics and relapsed heretics (those who after being pardoned a first serious offense, repeated the offense thus considered to have "relapsed into heresy") (qtd. in Clara Steinberg-Spitz).[24]

Despite the torture in Spain, Portugal, and the New World, the crypto-Jews and *conversos* lived on. Estimates of the number of Jews residing in New Spain should give us some idea of the magnitude of the descendant population today. Liebman's research estimates "that during the middle of the 17th century between two and three thousand Jews were living in New Spain. This is a considerable part of the total white population which, excluding the clerical hierarchy, is estimated at 20,000."[25] Hundreds of years later, we find multitudes of Sephardic descendants throughout the New World.

*Conversos* in the New World were destined to carry the secret of their heritage with them. The secret was passed down by their ancestors, disappearing in some cases, and continuing in others to this day, albeit in a diluted form. For those who retained vestiges of Judaism, there was a need for excessive secrecy. Family members often prayed in a dark room with drawn curtains, but their children were usually not privy to the rationale behind this secrecy.

Many *conversos* told of their families living in the mountains or hills of New Mexico, isolated, with no rabbis to teach them. Consequently, Jewish rituals were combined with those of the Church. Often, *conversos*, while still practicing Jewish rituals, became staunch Catholics, and remain so until this day. *Conversos* were not permitted to read Bibles, and according to some descendants, joining the Presbyterian Church, offered them the opportunity to read the Old Testament. At the same time, they were with their "own kind," people with their heritage. Above all, most of the individuals I interviewed consider themselves Catholic and Spanish. Many families insisted that their children remember a Spanish heritage from Spain and were quite adamant about not considering themselves Mexican, even though generations resided in areas of what is now Mexico. The descendants of Jews from Iberia brought their nationalistic feelings for Spain into modern times.

Recalling the successful documentation of his family from medieval Spain, José Antonio Esquibel writes:

> Both of my maternal grandparents are descendants of the Ha-Levi, Maluenda and Martínez de Lerma families of Burgos, Spain. These three families were prominent Jewish families that prospered in Castilian society as converts to Christianity. I can trace five lines of descent from these families to my maternal grandparents, mainly relying on sacramental records of the Catholic Church. The earliest of these is a baptismal record for my ancestor doña María Nuñez Ha-Levi, who was baptized in the Cathedral of Burgos on July 21, 1390, with her brothers, Rabbi Salomon (Selemoh) Ha-Levi and Alvar Ha-Levi, and her mother, doña María.. . . In my own family, there has been no memory of Jewish roots—no talk of being Jewish, nor any customs practiced by family members that resemble Jewish customs.[26]

Interestingly though, Jose's ancestors lived in Zacatecas and Nuevo León, among descendants of Jews from Spain, people with his background. Many Jews came to these areas because of the abundance of silver and "the development of silver mines."[27]

Guided to a village known for its crypto-Jewish inhabitants, I tried to establish connections with members of the community. After presenting an explanation for my presence, there was an eerie silence. Eye contact said much; there wouldn't be anyone to meet. I met a reporter who had written hundreds of articles—a worldly man who one would think was somewhat removed from his New Mexican roots. He too refused to be interviewed, as he had to consider the feelings of his family. Why is this still such a sensitive issue? Fear of the Inquisition is still in their thoughts, although the Mexican Inquisition was abolished in 1821. Another important factor for disguising their Jewish heritage is fear of being ostracized by friends, family, and the communities in which they live, where most people are Christian. It is also necessary to mention the Holocaust which served as a reminder of religious persecution in modern times, thus reinforcing the need, for many, to remain as they are, holding on to the secret of their Jewish ancestry.

According to most of the people interviewed, their families were endogamous; they married their own kind. Many families indicated that their marriages were arranged when they were quite young, and that they were often guided by their parents to marry within certain families. One woman's parents approved of a potential suitor by saying, "He is from a good family." That meant they were from the same people. Most families told of cousins marrying cousins, sometimes even first cousins. This was one way of keeping their Jewish practices hidden within the family structure. Often mentioned was that, "We're all related."

Emotions run high as the descendants of Sephardim reveal their Spanish or Portuguese heritage through photographs and oral histories presented in this publication. Witnessing history unravel through memory, one easily realizes how the spirit of a people and remnants of their heritage were preserved. Similar recollections recounted by so many people are sufficient evidence to support a story that must be told. Miraculously, descendants of Sephardim have survived with part of their heritage intact. Why? It is obvious to this interviewer that there exists a profound respect for all who came before them and all that was passed on by their ancestors.

Within the Hispanic communities of New Mexico and El Paso, Texas, we find descendants who are aware that some of the rituals they practiced were different than those practiced in Catholicism elsewhere.  In attempting to understand the reasons behind their religious practices, they feel compelled to research their heritage and determine if their ancestors converted from Judaism.  Whether they were literally forced to convert, or converted because of the political climate centuries ago, the effect was the same; much of their culture was lost.  For those with knowledge of a Jewish ancestry, there exists a need to trace their Jewish roots and understand what they have been practicing for so many generations.

Volumes speak of Judaism in the oral histories, either in memory or spirit.  Memories of that which was revealed through the years is truth to these people—memories of feelings, ideas, and practices within each family.  Or perhaps, as Erna Paris put it, "The year 1492 marked the end of their days in the Iberian peninsula, but for hundreds of years after, a memory of Spain clung to songs and fables crooned into the ears of the children from generation to generation."[28]

The oral histories collected in this book inform the reader of an important historical event through first-person recollections.  According to the Canadian Oral History Association, "For centuries the communication of historical information was exclusively oral.  Oral history refers to recorded interviews with individuals about the past, or first-person reminiscences."[29]  The oral histories, in this book, were obtained through first-person reminiscences.  The importance of oral history is unparalleled, as descendants of Sephardim are given a voice.

The British Library's National Sound Archive confirms: "In recent years oral history has emerged as a powerful means of recording and preserving the unique memories and life experiences of people whose stories might otherwise have been lost.  It enables us to eavesdrop on events, feelings, attitudes and ways of life which have been hidden from history, and thus create a more vivid and accurate picture of our past."[30]

Due to the sensitive nature of this project, it was often difficult to meet people willing to divulge their family history. The first person interviewed was Gerald González, introduced to me by a member of the Jewish Historical Society in New Mexico. Before each trip to New Mexico or El Paso, I would call synagogues, historical societies, universities, and former interviewees for introductions to people willing to come forward with their stories. Several people withdrew from my project as they reconsidered feelings of family members.

As each interview began, interviewees were provided with lists of Sephardic names that might be indicative of Sephardic ancestry. There are lists of names that might be attributed to descendants of Sephardim from Spain and Portugal. Many names have been traced to Inquisition records. According to Harry Stein of Sephardim.com, "*Conversos* did not really take names. They were assigned names by the church. Some *conversos* were forced to take the name of their sponsor, others the name of the town in which they were converted. Non-converted Jews also took names on their own as a matter of identification, Samuel de Aragón, Samuel de Toledo, Samuel de Sevilla, etc."[31] Also, families took names from nature. And some names changed in the course of moving from country to country. It is important to understand that a particular name does not in itself identify a descendant of Jews from the Iberian Peninsula.

The next step was to discuss rituals practiced within each family, comparing them to those practiced by crypto-Jews in Spain and Portugal, and thus compiling the story of the crypto-Jews in the New World. As mentioned in the appendix, many rituals find their origin in the Bible and define Judaism itself. Stories told by many participants in this project were sometimes quite revealing about an ancient Jewish heritage. Interviewer and interviewee were prepared for lengthy discussions, sometimes lasting several hours.

Most of the people interviewed either knew of their heritage or were suspicious of having a Jewish heritage. Those aware of their Jewish ancestry were clearly told by a family member, "We were Jews." Women in the family often revealed this Sephardic heritage to their children. They were the carriers of the faith. Renee Levine Melammed explains:

> The inquisitors realized the unusual importance of the home in crypto-Judaism and understood that the women willy-nilly became the carriers of the tradition that they viewed as inimical. The interactions between these women and their adversaries in court will reveal more than a mere list of judaizing activities; the determination of these women emerges and often triumphs over the "superior" power of the feared Holy Tribunal. As they themselves explained, although the mother might be burned at the stake, she would leave behind her children to carry on her teachings. [32]

Others *conversos* were informed about their Jewish heritage at the deathbed of a close relative. In Consuelo Luz's family, fifty years lapsed before passing on the truth of their Judaism.

Some descendants of *conversos* embrace their Sephardic heritage and presently attend synagogue services near their homes. Others feel torn, not knowing if they should return to Judaism or remain as they are. Satisfaction, for some individuals, often comes from discovering the truth of their ancestry, which adds another dimension to their identity. There are those who make it quite clear that they consider themselves Jews. Aware that their religion was forcibly taken away from them, the feeling expressed by some of the interviewees is that they should be accepted as Jews without having to go through a conversion process.

The story of the *conversos*, the crypto-Jews, and the *anusim* is a story that must be told as it has a distinct place in Jewish history. Five hundred years after the Edict of Expulsion, twenty-five generations later, what has become of the children through the centuries? What remains of their Judaism? This is explored in the oral histories presented in the pages that follow.

Living through the most difficult times, it is amazing to discover that after surviving centuries of persecution, forced conversions, and death, vestiges of Judaism still exist among descendants of Sephardim. Jewish practices were transferred from one generation to the next, mostly under the guise of Catholicism. Needless to say, much has been lost, but the voices heard in the oral histories will allow future generations to remember their ancestral home.

**I remain true to the words of the people interviewed.**

# NOTES

1. David M. Gitlitz, *Secrecy and Deceit: The Religion of the Crypto-Jews* (Philadelphia and Jerusalem: The Jewish Publication Society, 1996) 5.

2. Gitlitz 6.

3. Gitlitz 7.

4. Gitlitz 7.

5. Erna Paris, *The End of Days* (Amherst, NY: Prometheus Books, 1995) 247.

6. Paris 249.

7. Paris 249.

8. Paris 250.

9. Paris 251.

10. Paris 251.

11. Paris 250-51.

12. Paris 258.

13. Seymour B. Liebman, *New World Jewry, 1493-1825: Requiem for the Forgotten* (New York: KTAV Publishing House, 1982) 31.

14. Liebman, *New World Jewry* 17.

15. Liebman, *New World Jewry* 15.

16. Liebman, *New World Jewry* 19.

17. Liebman, *New World Jewry* 14.

18. Liebman, *New World Jewry* 19.

19. Liebman, *New World Jewry* 22.

20. Liebman, *New World Jewry* 23.

21. Dr. Seth Ward, "Sephardim and Crypto-Judaism: Definition of Terms and Brief History," University of Denver, 27 Nov. 2003 http://www.du.edu/~sward/sephardim.html.

22. Gitlitz 116.

23. Gitlitz 116.

24. Clara Steinberg-Spitz, "The Inquisition in the New World," *European Sephardic Institute* 1999, 26 Nov. 2003 http://www.sefarad.org/publication/lm/037/6.html.

25. Seymour B. Liebman, "The Jews of Colonial Mexico," *The Hispanic American Historical Review* 43.1 (1963): 100.

26. Jose Antonio Esquibel, e-mail to the author, 24 Feb. 2002.

27. Liebman, *New World Jewry* 52-53.

28. Paris 252.

29. Patricia Skidmore, "What Is Oral History?" *Canadian Oral History Association* 2002, 12 Nov. 2003 http://oral-history.ncf.ca/index.htm.

30. From http://www.bl.uk/collections/sound-archive/history.html with permission from the British Library Sound Archive (5 Nov. 2003).

31. Harry Stein, e-mail to the author, 18 May 2002.

32. Renee Levine Melammed, *Heretics or Daughters of Israel? The Crypto-Jewish Women of Castile* (New York: Oxford University Press, 1999) 15.

# Oral Histories

## Aaron Rael, Sr.

I was told that I had a Jewish heritage because of the name Rael. Gómez was a name in my mother's family. Our ancestor, Alonso Rael de Aguilar, came from Lorca, Spain, in 1683 through El Paso, Texas. He was a professional soldier in Spain, who came with de Vargas. He would help de Vargas reconquer New Mexico from the Indians in 1692.

The women wore black when a relative died and mourned for one year. They would light a candle on the one-year anniversary of a loved-one's death. There would also be a burial within twenty-four hours. During a burial they would throw dirt in the grave.

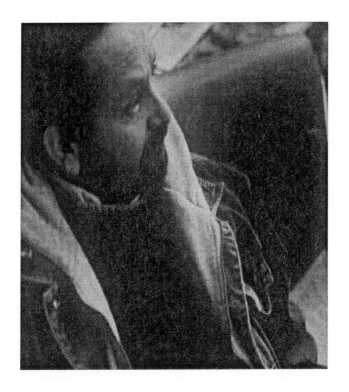

**Aaron Rael, Jr.**

The family practiced ritual slaughter where they would hang the animal upside down so that the blood would drain. Eggs with blood spots were avoided. During Passover, we made wheat flour which didn't rise. That was the unleavened bread for Passover. It was called *panocha*. The Penitentes did this. (The Penitentes were originally a lay order, which took the place of the Franciscan priests who were sent to Spain.) They went underground around 1847, and have been a very secretive group since.

Penitentes means "Brotherhood of Light." The women sit separately from the men in their house of worship.

I played a game called *pon y saca*, similar to the dreidel game. Grandmother knew it, and Dad knows it. The family ate *empanaditas* at Christmas. If any food fell to the floor, they would put the sign of the cross on it.

Questa is the furthest northern settlement of Colonial Spain. We really believe that we have a Jewish heritage, but some things are derivative of the Indian culture. Questa was settled because they did not put Spaniards here.

*Conversos* believe that's why Jews came. *Mestizos* (a mixture of whites and Indians) came here too. There is a three-part history of the Jews in the area: I. Colonization, 2. Constant Warfare, 3. Alliances with the Native Americans.

**Lydia Peña-Abelicio Márquez-Peña (Abe Peña) (Sister and Brother)**

## Abe

Peña means rock.

My wife and I became friendly with a Peace Corp couple in Costa Rica—his name was Don Goldman. He served as a Peace Corp volunteer assisting the Costa Ricans in setting up a national park service. He would probe at me about Judaism. It stimulated my interest to pursue that I might be of Jewish descent. In Washington, we met with them and they took us to a *bat mitzvah*. When I left the synagogue, I said, "You know, I felt like I had been through that experience once before." This again peaked my curiosity. I came home and consulted professors at the University of New Mexico about the crypto-Jews, thinking our background may have gone back to the Jews in Spain.

When visiting a grave, I kind of remember leaving a rock on top of a pile of dirt. If we went to visit people in their homes and they weren't there, we would find a rock or two and leave it by the threshold to indicate we were there. Our parents said we came from Spain, through Mexico and eventually here to New Mexico. They came in 1598 with Oñate.

Our ancestors were not concerned with history. They were concerned with survival, which revolved around the Catholic connection. As an adult in Costa Rica, I heard for the first time from a professor of the University of Costa Rica that we might be Jewish. Names in the family are Peña, Márquez, Ortega, Chávez, Ortiz, and Gutiérrez.

Growing up, the community was pretty much related. Third and more cousins could marry. Anglos said our Spanish was different. In college, I was told that I spoke a more archaic Spanish. We were active churchgoers. My sister, Lydia, is a nun. We had a twenty-four hour burial. We prayed with rosaries at night while the casket was built.  There was a one-year mourning period.

A few days after a person's burial, we visited the family that suffered the loss to offer our sympathies.  We did this within one week. It was called to *dar el pesar* or *dar el pésame.*

Members of the family and others who attended the funeral threw a handful of dirt in the grave.  After the people were gone, other relations filled it up.  Tombstones generally had crosses on them.  Hispanic cemeteries until 1950 had very few granite headstones.

Grants is west of Albuquerque.  The first settlement west of Albuquerque was Seboyeta in the 1800s.  They came from Albuquerque with oxen.  There was no evidence of Stars of David in this area of western New Mexico.  One thing I remember about Grandmother was that she would take salt when there was lightning and recite the Prayer of Santa Barbara.  Then she threw salt that would apparently minimize the effects of the thunder or discourage the lightning from striking us.

When slaughtering sheep, we would hang the sheep by its hind legs from a pole in the corral.  We'd pull her up about eighteen inches and then take a sharp knife, make a cross—followed by a quick cut.  We would say, *Jesús y Cruz* (Jesús and the Cross).  I was a meat inspector in the army.  The rabbi would say a prayer for anything that would go to the Jewish troops.  This may have been a throwback to Judaism. We saved the blood in a pail, and Mother would make a dish and add chicken.  With chickens, we'd grab two legs and cut the neck with a sharp ax.  We salted meat if it was made into jerky.  The salt was used to shoo flies away and add flavor.

At one time, when women had babies, they stayed in the house about thirty days.  During Lent, we ate *panocha*  and blue corn *tortillas*.  Most of the activity was around the *morada* during Holy Week.  Villagers brought food to the *morada* during the week of Easter. Easter Sunday was the last day of Lent. We ate *sopapillas* most of the time. They were deep-fried. We ate more *sopapillas* during Christmas and more blue corn *tortillas* during Lent.

We were not encouraged to read the Old Testament and didn't even read the New Testament. We had a Bible at home but were not encouraged to read it. We were so segregated in the village of San Mateo that we grew up without prejudices and listened to the radio. We were children of people from Northern New Mexico. One of the sources of information was the priest. We asked the priest questions. Our early education was from the priests. Mother fed priests after mass. Education was very important in the family. Our grandparents were church oriented.

Mom and Dad were distant cousins— third cousins. The family came through Vera Cruz, to Mexico City, north to Zacatecas. We believe they spent one generation in Zacatecas. They crossed the Rio Grande and settled in San Gabriel, near Española. San Gabriel no longer exists. Our father was born December 28, 1898. We have a family tradition where we meet as a family on his birthday. We pay for a mass at a local Catholic Church on the 28th. Generally, other families do the same.

Birth dates and deaths are very important in our family. The year anniversary of the death is important in our family. We pray and reflect. Mom said, "Don't bury me in black." She didn't like black. This may have been a throwback to Judaism. We had to wear black if a close member of the family died.

I believe I have this heritage. Whenever I go to Jewish services, I feel I'm in there.

**Lydia**

I believe strongly that we have a Jewish heritage. I go to a *Seder* dinner every year. What felt very good was that the whole family was participating. The father was leading us in prayer, and that's the tradition that we had.

A woman down the street wanted Mother to bless her. She asked Mother and not me (I'm a nun and was standing there). My mother felt humbled. The woman said, "I want you to bless me and pray over me and place your hands on my head." We do it in Loretto. Growing up, the elders would bless us. We would kneel, and they placed their hands on our heads. Children observed Sunday as the day of rest in San Mateo. People visited one another.

Sometimes the family would take water and bless us with the sign of a cross on our forehead. This is not done in church.

**Albert Gallegos**

I discovered information about my heritage after having traveled to Spain eleven times, meeting people and asking questions. Visiting friends in Granada, Spain, I was told that the name Gutiérrez is Jewish. My friend, whose last name is

Gutiérrez, informed me that he is Jewish. Another family name on the maternal side of the family is Salas, a Jewish name. Although not proven, I have been told that Gallegos is a Jewish name. I found this out from a tour guide in Sevilla, Spain. He said Gallegos is a Jewish name from northern Spain.

Growing up, I never thought of it. Nothing gave me any inclination that we were Jewish. My grandparents and parents said, "Your heritage is Spanish." They were adamant about remembering our heritage. They probably didn't know if we were Jewish. The family was very Catholic, and a church was built on our property. They buried the family under the church, which was their own cemetery, or immediately right outside the church. There is a tombstone in the family cemetery on the property with the name Trujillo that has a Star of David on it. It is an old sandstone one, and it's hand carved.

The family blessed the children by placing their hands on their heads and making the sign of the cross. Blessings were given on special occasions, if you were leaving, going on a trip, getting married, or having a birthday.

In the old days, when Grandfather died, Grandmother wore black. They lit candles on the year anniversary of the deceased back then. Handfuls of dirt were thrown on the coffin as it was lowered into the grave. There were flowers as well.

We didn't believe in circumcision. There weren't many icons in our home and the family was not secretive. My grandmothers were Gonzáles and Padilla. They prayed at altars set in their bedroom and prayed in Spanish. They prayed the rosary. They didn't pray in church because we lived about forty or fifty miles from the church. The priest would come to the area once a month.

There weren't many people where we lived. Mostly everyone is related to one another.

When I went on a trip to northern Spain, I was told by people we visited, that the Spanish we were speaking was old Castilian Spanish. We still speak that Spanish and the people of northern New Mexico primarily do so as well.

Nobody avoided church in our family. There weren't any Penitentes on Father's side. In my family, on Mother's side, my aunts were married to Penitentes.

Education was very important in our family. It was important going back to my grandparents, great-grandparents, and great-great-grandparents.

The Gallegos family came with Cortéz and entered the New World through Cuba. They stayed there awhile before coming to Mexico, Mexico City, and then north. It's documented that most of Cortéz's people came through Cuba. Those who came with Cortéz were military people. I don't definitely know if anyone is Jewish.

On Father's side, on some occasions, cousins married cousins. This didn't happen too often and stopped around 1910. Marriages were generally arranged for the purpose of keeping status and wealth within the family. The family wanted us to marry within our own. This didn't happen on Mother's side.

We ate *empanaditas*, which contained meat and raisins, during Christmas. *Quelites* were eaten during their season of growth which was in the spring.

Our family attends church. As I grew up, I learned at home to believe in one God, the Father Almighty, Creator of Heaven and Earth. I learned that when I was a little kid. We believed in the teachings of the Catholic Church. We weren't religious growing up and attended mass once a month. The Gallegos grandparents read the Old Testament. It doesn't feel important that I find out if I'm Jewish. I'm interested in genealogy and interested in the truth. I'm not emotional about it.

## Ambrosia González

My maiden name was Ortiz. Mom's family was Ortega. Dad's family was Ortiz and Archuleta. When Dad asked his family where we came from, his parents told him that we were from Spain. Grandma, on Mom's side, was Irish. Mom said, "The Lord is one."

We believed in circumcision as the doctor advised it. This

was done about a week after the baby was born. All my kids were circumcised except the last one.

Dad raised animals and ate the blood. We wouldn't do it now because the Bible says not to. Eggs with blood spots were thrown out.

We had a twenty-four hour burial. Coins were placed on the eyes of the deceased. People would visit right after the funeral. We had a one-year mourning period for Grandma. Mom covered the mirrors when someone died. Grandma prayed every night and knelt down every night to say a prayer with the rosary. She prayed in the bedroom by herself and was very quiet about it. No one knew when she would do it. She covered her head with a black shawl (*tapado*) when she went to church.

Dad's cousin went to Spain to look for the name Ortiz. The name was not found in Spain. Instead he found the name Ortz. Dad's cousin, Alfredo Ortiz, said that when they came over they changed a vowel or put in a vowel because they were afraid of persecution. I think they were afraid of being identified as Jews.

During Holy Week, we didn't do anything for three days. We couldn't play. We made *panocha*. It didn't have yeast and didn't rise. *Buñuelos* were fried *tortillas*, round and rolled, and were eaten once in a while. Mom swept away from the door. She put a dustpan in the middle of the kitchen. I remember when it rained; they threw salt out and made a cross. My brother couldn't drink milk when he was growing up, as he was lactose intolerant. He had pasteurized milk.

We were told that we spoke *mochos* Spanish. We spoke English and Spanish. Our Spanish wasn't considered correct. We have been told that our Spanish is different. Our Spanish was probably lost along the way. When candles were lit we didn't know what they were for.

I know I am Jewish because of the crypto-Jewish meeting. Upon returning from one of these meetings, I asked my dad, "Where did we come from?" He said we came from Spain. He told me about a game called *chuecos* played with a long pole on a horse. When I was small we played *trompos*. Dad said it came from Spain. It was like a spinning top. The letters on it were P *(Pon)*, meaning put in, S *(Saca)*, meaning take out amount put in, T *(Todo)*, meaning take whole thing, and N *(Nada)*, meaning nothing. Dad said this came from Spain.

I read a book about Columbus, which said Jews ate a lot of garlic and onions. It was called *Sails of Hope*. It also said that the tribes of Judah and Benjamin came from Spain.

I feel strongly that I'm from the tribe of Judah or Benjamin because of what I heard at a crypto-Jewish conference. I'm a Born Again Christian now. I'm trying to find out about Jewish rituals.

I visited my aunt, and she said her grandma, my great-grandmother, said we're from Spain.

**Ana Kurland**

I was told when I was very little that our ancestors were Jews. It was superficial talk, and I think it was meant to show that we were Spanish and not the regular Puerto Rican mix.

Mom's family has the most. My great-grandparents came from Spain to Puerto Rico in the mid 1800s. They were *conversos* and practiced one-half Catholicism and one-half Judaism.

The first thing I noticed was a big celebration on New Year's Day, when I was eight years old. I asked why we have a New Year's celebration when everyone else (school friends) celebrated Christmas. Christmas celebration was minor. I was told it was my grandfather's saint's day. Being a good

Catholic school girl, I went to a saint's day book. Grandfather's name was Manuel. I didn't find St. Manuel anywhere. My mother kept insisting on that reason for this holiday. I asked an aunt. She said that was the day of Jesús' circumcision. To this day, she denies saying this.

My grandparents were Ana and Manuel. Mom is Ana. My sister is Ana. My grandmother is Ana. All of my female cousins are Ana. All the boys are Manuel, used as a middle name. I was told on the Internet that this was a custom used for protection against the Inquisition. If the Inquisition came to a house and wanted, for example, Ana Moreno, they couldn't take you because they didn't know which one you were. The Inquisition kept precise records. There is no proof of this custom.

There weren't any crucifixes, saints, altars, or pictures of Jesús in our house. We were told that the priests were drunks and liars within the family. We never went to church, not Christmas or Easter, even though I went to Catholic school. My family came to San Juan from Galicia in Spain. It was a Celtic area. Mom had red hair and hazel eyes.

I think my aunt who told us about circumcision was assigned to carry on the story of our heritage. When I was twelve, I had a crisis of faith and stopped believing in Catholicism. I researched other religions and didn't like most. I read about Judaism and couldn't find anything to eliminate it. I studied twelve years, took classes and read on my own. Then I decided to convert. I am a practicing Jew now. My husband was born an Ashkenazi Jew. The rest of the family has not converted. As long as I believe in God, they'll leave me alone.

It is possible Mom was not told about our heritage. When I converted, Mom told my godfather, and he thought it was great. There were certain lists of families that were okay to marry up to my grandparents' generation. If there was intermarriage with Indians or Africans, they would rather they married Spanish Catholics.

My brothers were not circumcised. Our parents were secretive. They never prayed to Jesús. It was always Father God. They never prayed to the Virgin Mary or saints. They never mentioned the Trinity. I didn't go to Sunday school. I went to Catholic school because that was the best education. We worked Saturday and Sunday.

Grandmother's mother died when Grandmother was thirteen. A lot of things didn't get passed on. After birth, women stayed in the house forty days.

We were told about the Old Testament by Mom. Children's names in the family are Old Testament names and only Old Testament names going back generations— Manuel, Joseph, Angel, Rachel, Anibel, Elizabeth.

Mom said the Old Testament was better than the New Testament. New Year's Day was the only time of no work.

We would eat roast calf on a spit in Puerto Rico. It was common to roast a pig on Christmas Day. Christmas, as we grew up, became less and less important. When I was very little, women wore Spanish *mantillas* in church until about 1965. It was a Catholic thing, but the Catholic Church stopped doing that. My oldest aunt might know something but won't say. She denies telling me about circumcision or the reason for celebrating New Year's. I think that I found my soul. I knew it was right and felt it.

**Ana María Martínez and Grace Luján (Sisters)**

**Ana María**

Up until five years ago, I never thought of having any Jewish roots.  My second son brought me an article on Sephardic Jews in New Mexico.  It mentioned some last names, and both my mother's maiden name, Lucero, as well as my dad's last name, Valencia, were on that list. I read it and set it aside. Then in October of 1999, I went to Spain and a historian told me Valencia was Jewish.  So now I'm interested in finding out a little more about Jewish customs to see if there are any comparisons in our foods and some religious rituals.

My sister, Grace Luján, and my daughter, María, have been attending Adat Yeshua and have claimed some similarities which I remember happening in our childhood, such as lighting a candle or two as we prayed in the evening.  Our day started with and ended in prayer.

When someone passed away, the mirrors were covered with black cloth, people brought food, and store owners sent large boxes of groceries. The ladies from the community came and helped cook, so the relatives could visit with the people that came all through the day and night to pay their respects and offer their love and support to the grieving family. Everyone that came was fed.

Someone remained with the body after midnight when everyone left, and chanted prayers during the early morning hours, at the break of dawn.

Some Jewish foods that we ate were stuffed cabbage leaves, but since I'm not familiar with traditions, it will be interesting for me to find out as I study more about the Jewish traditions.

Although I am interested in finding out more, I know I will appreciate and be proud if I do have Jewish roots, but I will continue in my Catholic faith because it's what I was raised in. It's what my ancestors practiced for many years back. I know I'll support my sister and my daughter and respect their beliefs.

**Grace Luján**

My husband and I were living in southern California and had Messianic teachings. We became interested in this teaching and learned a lot of Judaism.

I'd come to New Mexico and question my mom on traditions and also food she would prepare. There were traditions in the family such as covering mirrors while in mourning, not eating fish such as catfish, putting stones on graves, and placing a handful of dirt into the grave after the coffin was in.

Dad took out a dreidel.

Mom cooked on Friday, and we didn't do anything on the weekends.

I feel a very great connection to Judaism, especially attending services on Saturdays. This is very special to me. I feel completed and have a special feeling inside of me, like a peace.

Grandpa read the Bible to us, mainly the Old Testament.

I asked God if I was Jewish, to show me in some way. Well, I had forgotten about this. When in Israel at the airport, a Jewish man standing in a booth motioned to me to come over where he was. My son, Daniel, was with me and said to me, "Mom he just wants to sell you something." I said I couldn't be rude so I walked over to him, and my son followed. This man said to me, "You're Jewish," and smiled and turned to my son, "and your mother is Jewish so you're Jewish." I was surprised and remembered my prayer; it was awesome!

**Anselmo Arellano**

Rivera is Mom's last name. I know that my ancestors are from the Basque province of Navarra and the small community of Arellano in Spain. This area is near the Pyrenees mountain range between Spain and France. The first Arellano came to New Mexico in 1695. Juan Cristóbal de Arellano was a captain in the Spanish Army. He served as the *alcalde* (mayor) of different communities, including Albuquerque, Bernalillo, and Santa Cruz. I am directly descended from him. Since only one Arellano, Juan Cristóbal, came to New Mexico during the Spanish period, all northern New Mexicans with the name Arellano are descended from him. There was one other Arellano who came, and he was a priest.

Riveras and Arellanos were suspected of being secret Jews by the Office of the Holy Inquisition in Mexico City. The Inquisition in the New World did not invoke punishments as severe as those in Spain. Those accused of being Sephardic Jews were basically given a slap on the hand. Many of those accused did colonize northern New Mexico since 1598. The surnames appear in those records found in Mexico City.

We twirled the chicken until it was decapitated. We soaked and salted meat. We use the term *sudario* as a type of prayer. According to a rabbi in Santa Fe, this is a Jewish word for prayer. We have always been full-fledged Catholics. My father said, "There is only one God. The Lord is one."

During the Spanish Colonial and Mexican periods, sheepherders and other travelers in New Mexico were killed by Indians or thieves. People would travel by mule, donkey, or on foot. During that time, travelers would leave a stone at the site where a person had been killed. Eventually, a small mound of stones would develop. They are known as *descansos*, or the resting place of a departed soul. It meant you said a prayer for the soul of the departed and left a stone to symbolize your stop and spiritual offering. This tradition continues today, but families place a crucifix where someone has died, usually for someone killed in an automobile accident.

During the Spanish and Mexican periods, we had twenty-four hour burials. The body was wrapped in the nicest blanket a person owned; this was before coffins. There weren't coffins because lumber was non-existent in New Mexico before 1846. Sawmills came after. We were told our Spanish is a little different, and it is. It's archaic from the sixteenth century.

I do believe many northern New Mexicans have some Jewish ancestry, just like we have from many other races, including the last ones we came in contact with, the Native Americans.

## Antonio Francisco Gallegos

Dad's name was José Absolón Gallegos. We are practicing Catholics. I know of the Hebrew names through research. Absolón was probably the Spanish equivalent of Absalom, the name of King David's or King Solomon's son. Dad was born in 1906.

My grandfather, on Dad's side, was born in 1864. My great-grandfather was José Ramón Gallegos. He had a son José Abraham Gallegos. I believe Dad was circumcised. He looked Jewish. He was about six feet tall and had a Jewish-type nose.

The Roybal line has Jewish ancestry. The first Roybal was married to a woman whose name was Gómez Robledo. Francisco, her father, was tried by the Inquisition for practicing

Jewish ritual. He was called a crypto-Jew and was acquitted. My great-great-grandmother, Rosalia de Gracia Roybal, was born in 1826. Grandmother was María Juana Roybal. Mom was María Librada (I suspect it means liberated in Hebrew) Gonzáles. Gonzáles always had an s at the end. The Gonzáles side goes back to Coimbra, Portugal. It goes back to Diego Blanden, born Gonzáles in 1559. Luján goes back to the Canary Islands.

Grandmother, María Josefa Luján, is on Mother's side. Her husband was Fermín Gonzáles. Juan José Luján was born in 1573 in La Palma, Canary Islands. It was a matriarchal system in that area. The men would take the mother's last name. Sometimes it happened in New Mexico. Juan José Luján was the first one who came to New Mexico. His father was Rodríguez.

Jewish ancestry probably comes with the sixth great-grandfather, Francisco Gómez Robledo, born in 1643. He came from Calda de Reyes in Galicia, Spain. In my case, this is the only documented case where Francisco Gómez Robledo, born in Portugal, was accused of being a Jew in New Mexico. He went to Mexico City to stand trial and was cleared of charges. He didn't come back, but his daughters or granddaughters came back to New Mexico. Any Jewish ancestry is traced to Gómez and Robledo.

My brother is Eloy, the Spanish version of the Hebrew name Eloi. Both Mom and Dad are Catholics. They told us who we were—Spanish (*Españoles*), meaning from Spain. Mexico gained independence from Spain between 1840 and 1848. Then they called themselves Spanish Americans *(Españoles Americanos* or *Americanos)*. They thought they were from Spain. They never considered themselves Mexican.

Some families came through Vera Cruz. That was the only port where Spain allowed people to come in. Anyone who came had to be cleared by the Inquisition. They didn't want Jews or Protestants. If they had been Jewish, they were *conversos. Conversos* were allowed to come. Protestants came around the 1840s.

I'm Catholic because I'm comfortable with it and I believe in it. There was secretiveness with me. Mom and Dad were devout Catholics and liked pictures of saints and statues in the house and went to church. I'm the same. When Antonio was asked why he was doing this genealogy, his reply was, "I'm doing this genealogy because I'm tired of reading about people telling me from whom I came without documenting the facts."

As for mourning practices, we had a *velorio*. People would come and pray the rosary the first night, along with other prayers. They had mass the next morning followed by a burial and eulogy. We ate after the burial. People came to visit up to a year after the burial. There weren't any dances. On the one-year anniversary, the priest offered a mass for the deceased.

I was told that my Spanish was different from Spanish spoken in Spain and that we used old words, ancient words. I use idioms that came from Spain, and they could understand me. In Mexico, they said we spoke differently. Mom and Dad avoided eating blood. My wife and daughter don't eat eggs with blood spots because they don't like to see raw blood. I don't either.

When slaughtering animals, they slit the throat and hung the animal to drain the blood. A sharp knife was used. I never saw Dad eat or prepare anything with blood. We twirled the chicken until it was decapitated.

*Panocha*s were eaten during Holy Week and Christmas. *Buñuelos* were made during Christmas and all the time. During Christmas we made *empanaditas* that were meat-filled pastries. The ingredients included pinon nuts, raisins, sugar, and sweet meats that were placed inside the flour. It was fried.

We were told to "Keep the *Sabbath* holy." We didn't work. It was a day of rest. The *Sabbath* was followed on Sunday. Dad would pray in bed privately after everyone went to bed. He would pray in Spanish. He was a very private man. Only Father did this. Mother would pray wherever she was. She wasn't as private as my dad. Dad's mother was very quiet and good.

There were practices followed in the family without explanation. When going into the bathtub, Dad and Mom would touch water with their right hand and touch the top of our forehead. I did it as a child and didn't know why it was done. They would say, "*Moja la morilla.*" (Wet the forehead.) To me it had some religious significance, something to do with blessing of water.

Mother had a fear of gypsies. She called them *Turcos*. She thought they might steal us. If my grandmother saw them coming, she would go out and grab us. They claimed that if you looked at the baby too much, you would give him the bad eye. It would curse him.

My sister and my son are lactose intolerant. The Gómez part of the family (Francisco and his brother) had something called *Las Colitas*. According to the records, they had a little tail, an extension on the tail bone. That apparently had some Jewish significance, but I don't know. I suspect I have a Jewish heritage. The Roybals owned stores, were wealthy, and looked Jewish. We went to Bible classes to read the Old Testament and spoke of catechism. Dad read both the Old and New Testaments. I read excerpts from Exodus and Genesis in church. Catholics were not encouraged to read the Bible because they might misinterpret it. Now we can read it. We lived on a land grant in the surrounding area with all family members. We knew with whom we should associate because others were different and their upbringing was different. I married within the family. Mom and Dad were fourth cousins.

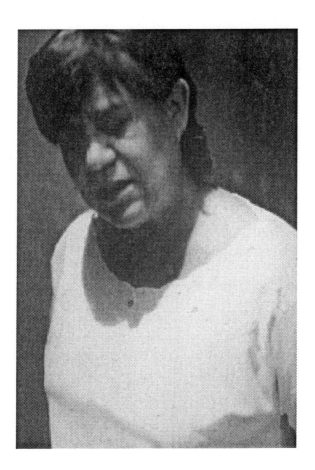

Linda Armas

Approximately thirteen years ago, two cousins did an extensive genealogy search and traced maternal lines to Jewish heritage. Since then, I have gone into the Internet and checked for any other evidence using my paternal lines. I did find that my father's maternal last name "Villarreal" originally had the Star of David on its family crest, indicative of their heritage. We also have several first names in our family traditional to the Jewish heritage such as Emma, David, Gloria, Saul, and Samuel.

Jewish rituals practiced in my home, or by other members of my family:  Perhaps the most common was the covering of mirrors (as well as turning the saints/icons to face the wall or by covering them) when there was a death in the family.

We were baptized on Saturdays.  We lit candles on a loved one's death anniversary.  We prayed with family and friends for seven days after the death of a loved one, and the immediate relatives maintained mourning for one year.

We lit a *menorah* at Christmas.  We would butcher by hanging the carcass upside down and allowing the blood to completely drain from the animal.  We kissed bread or *tortilla* if it fell to the floor (we could eat it afterward).

Yes, I feel a connection to Judaism.  On a rational level, it had been difficult for me to understand why.  I used to feel it was primarily curiosity of the unknown, or disillusionment with my present beliefs.

## Carlos Maximiliano Casaus

My father selected me as "The Rememberer" to pass on the oral history of his family. All my information is from my father. Great-Grandmother wouldn't talk about it. Father's family has been in New Mexico since 1635.

Pedro de las Casas came to the New World with Columbus on his second voyage. Columbus was friendly with de las Casas. He offered to bring him to America, and they settled here. Why would my forefathers be friendly with Columbus? They were probably the same people or were related. They came to Santo Domingo, at that time called Isabela. Why did they come? They were convinced by the discovery of a new land, and they came for a better life. He came with his family.

There were three brothers Casaus who were originally from France. The brothers volunteered their services to the King of Spain in order to get rid of the Moors. The Moors were defeated and sent from Spain to Africa. Two of the brothers died in the war. One survived the war and was given a title. The name was changed from Casaus to de las Casas. Casas was a titled name. Pedro's grandson married the daughter of Moctezuma. I did not know, at this time, if there was a Jewish history from Spain in the family. My ancestors lived in the southern part of Mexico and had lots of property. The area is now called the state of Chiapas in Mexico. Centuries later, an Indian became president of Mexico. He didn't want Jews or Spaniards in Mexico. Our people decided to escape the killing that would be done by the president of Mexico. They were given one year to depart, and so they came in the 1600s, before 1635, to New Mexico. In the meantime, the name was changed back to Casaus.

When I was a child, I found out from Carlos, my father, that we had Jewish blood. Father told me that Great-Grandmother Teresa Sena, his grandmother, has Jewish blood from her Grandfather Peresh. I was told that Peresh is a Jewish name from Spain. Father said Peresh was a *Marrano*. There are no written records of this information. Peresh was a grandfather on her father's side. Peresh had a cart with two horses and sold spices to Mexicans before 1840. He was a lonely man. He or his children changed the name to Pérez because of wanting to be Mexican and hiding their Jewish origin. The name Peresh had a Jewish connotation in Spain. We don't know where Peresh came from, except that he was a Jew and called a *Marrano*. Peresh married a Spanish woman with Spanish ancestry. On Great-Grandmother Sena's maternal side, her mother's last name was Terrazas.

Teresa Sena and Great-Grandfather Carlos Casaus raised me in my early years. I was the first great-grandson. There I learned Spanish with the Mexicans and the Indians. My father spoke English because he wanted his children to be Americans.

When it stormed, Great-Grandmother Sena lit a candle to

a saint, kneeled, and prayed to be spared from the dangerous storm and lightning. She would tell me, "Carlitos, go under my bed and bring out the box." The box was about twenty-four by thirty inches. She would take out a seven-candle *menorah* and light the candles. We all had to kneel down and pray to the *menorah*. I asked, "What are we praying to and why do you light seven candles?" She said, "We are praying to the seven Catholic sacraments." I responded, "Grandma, you have all saints and religious objects on walls. Why do you keep religious objects under the bed?" She answered, "because my mother told me to." Why would she hide it? She was very secretive. I recognized that Great-Grandma's brother had red hair. Father explained, "That's because they're Jewish."

Mom's Family: My mother said that her Great-Grandfather Gallegos was a Spaniard and came from Galicia. He committed a crime in Galicia. He worked in a slaughterhouse, found a wife, and left for America. He was afraid of being caught for the crime. They knew they were coming to America and landed in New Orleans. They probably came around 1775, directly from Spain. Mother's father was a Gallegos. Mother's mother was a Sandoval. Mother was Isabel Gallegos, and she married Casaus. Her forefathers came from Spain and were blond and blue-eyed. We didn't know if they were Jewish. Grandma Sandoval's great-grandfather was the man for whom Sandoval County in New Mexico was named. We don't claim other Sandovals as relatives, but some do exist. Sandovals are Mom's relatives. Grandma Sandoval married Isidoro Gallegos. As for biblical names, there was a relative with the name Moisés.

We buried the dead the next day. I asked why and was told the body would deteriorate very fast. We placed coins on the eyes of the deceased to keep them closed. After burial, they would sit one or two days, and people would come with food. I avoided funerals but didn't know why.

After a time, all relatives would go to the priest and pay

him a certain sum of money to say a prayer in favor of the dead person. He would mention the name of the deceased. This was done on the one-year anniversary of a person's death. An ad would be placed in the obituary column of a newspaper on the one-year anniversary of a loved-one's death for a few years. The purpose of this was to remind relatives and people known to the deceased of his death. You can still see these ads in newspapers.

Mother's brothers were very intelligent, and I have always felt (in my family) that intelligence was tied up with being Jewish. The family owned land, and we had workers (Mexicans and Indians) who called me "The Mexican Jew."

We did light bonfires before Christmas. I don't know why.

We used a special knife to slaughter animals. We would cut the throat of a lamb and drain the blood into a cup until it was filled. We would also twirl a chicken until it was decapitated. We salted some meat (beef).

After birth, the woman would stay in the house for a long time. She was not allowed to bathe, uncover herself, or change clothes. About eight days after the birth of a boy, a prayer was said in Spanish.

We were told that our Spanish was archaic, Ladino. My Grandfather Casaus said that I spoke Ladino. Mother's mother spoke Ladino. We actually shifted between Mexican Spanish and Ladino. Ladino was from Mother's family.

We avoided pork. Dad never had a pig on the ranch, but he had lambs, hens, and turkeys. We were told that the reason for not having pigs was that the pigs were fed scrap, and they were dirty.

We were wealthy and owned houses. Before *Yom Kippur*, we went to our house in the mountains. It had forested land.

We went in the summertime for a three- or four-day trip. This was a short time before the High Holy Days. We had picnics in the mountains and said prayers before and after the food was eaten. Mom didn't know why we did it. If she did, she didn't mention it. The term High Holy Days was not known to me until after I joined the army.

During Holy Week (March), before Passover, we ate *capirotada*. We also had round crackers, for the unleavened bread, which were eaten with pudding. Passover, the name, became known to me later on. I started realizing that we had more Jewish ancestry than we knew.

After Christ's return from the dead (Easter Day), we would use noisemakers and go around the outside of the church, twirling them, around and around. We would also attend church. This was when I was young. *Empanadas* were eaten at this time. They were filled with a meat and fruit mixture.

Women covered their heads in church. Mom was superstitious, and believed certain foods would make us ill. We didn't eat the innards of pigs, pork, heart, or liver. Others ate this.

A pregnant woman, Great-Grandmother Sena's relatives, would place a key on her stomach to insure that she would have a healthy birth. This practice also was to serve another purpose, and that was to bring on labor. She would stand by the doorway, with the moon shining and the key on her stomach. We don't know the reason for the key or the significance of the moon. This was a superstitious practice. I don't feel a connection to Judaism.

### Cecilia Gallegos

My maiden name was Sena. In 1694, a childless couple came to Santa Fe from Mexico, more than likely descendants from Spain. This childless couple brought a nine-year-old boy, Bernardino Sena, who claimed to be an orphan. In those days, a childless couple could not become colonists in New Mexico, so they adopted Bernardino to complete the family. When this family came in 1694, they settled in Santa Fe in what is now known as Santa Fe Plaza. A plaque in the park indicates that this was true because it names Bernardino Sena and the year he came. As far as I know, we come from Bernardino's lineage on Father's side. He was twenty years old when he got married in Poquaque, New Mexico, and had to name his parents on the marriage certificate. Assuming his parents were still alive, he named them. People in the family have researched that we are descended from Bernardino Sena. I think it was a plan of his parents to send him with good people so he could have a better life. Bernardino grew up to be wealthy. He was reared in a savvy way. They indoctrinated him with success and guidance. He got to be the owner of part of Santa Fe that is now Bernardino Sena Plaza, in the main area of Santa Fe.

Mom's side (her father's side):  They became Gurule (Mother's father's side) in Albuquerque, New Mexico. Gurule was Mom's maiden name.  In France it was Grolet, but changed in Albuquerque.  Grandfather, on Mom's side, was French.  (We also have a Spanish heritage on Mom's side.)  They came from Spain.  Gene Archi Beck and Jaques Grolet came to Mexico through Canada in the 1700s.  Prior to going to Mexico they were enslaved by the Indians (the latter part of the 1600s).  Indians had them hunt for them.  The Indians trusted them, and they allowed themselves to be trusted because they had a plan to escape. I think they came here to make money.  They made their way to Albuquerque.

Jaques Grolet was my grandfather's ancestor who came from France.  My grandfather is a descendant of Jaques Grolet.  In Albuquerque, he met up with a young lady, Elena Gallegos, a wealthy lady.  She was an only child and they fell in love.  This is according to what my mom used to tell me. He had to change his name in order to marry Elena Gallegos because he was French and she was a full-blooded Spaniard. Her father said there is only one way you can marry my daughter and that is to change your name to a Spanish name— Gurule.  Many people in the family today sign their original name Grolet.

The Elena Land Grant was donated to the town of Albuquerque and is being used as a park. It is called the Elena Land Grant Park.  Jaques Gurule and Elena had one son, Tomás Gurule.  That's where the Gurule started.  Tomás had a large family.

Jaques was called Santiago. I'm derived from Jaques on Mom's father's side.  Cecilio Gurule was Mom's dad, and he married Felipa Delgado.  They came for gold and a better life. There was never evidence of Judaism.  Felipa Delgado,

Mom's mother and my grandmother came from a province in Spain. They went to Mexico and then to New Mexico like her dad's side.

Manuel Delgado was a captain in the Spanish army. He was my great-great-great-grandfather. He married Josefa García de Noriega. They got married in Juarez, Mexico. After Manuel, came Estanislado, son of Manuel, and then came Juan Pablo, Mother's grandfather and son of Estanislado. He married Trinidad Lucero de Godoy.

Manuel was a Spanish soldier. The Mexican government sent him and his family along with other soldiers and their families to establish and settle Santa Fe as the capital of New Mexico. They came in the latter 1700s or 1800s. They were still fighting Indians every day. There were constant battles.

This is all on Mom's side. We were never told about Judaism. We were very strong Catholics, and it is very possible that Franciscan priests were here converting people to Catholicism.

On Mom's side there were no biblical names. Mom said, "The Lord is the only one."

We rested on Sunday. My dad liked to barter. Friends would come and trade mostly on Sunday. Very early in the morning, Mom would cook a special dinner and we would take it to the mountains where we would enjoy the meal. We would pray. That was a time we could take more time about our prayers, in Spanish. Mom would teach us catechism, without interruptions, so that we could make our first Holy Communion. All Catholic families taught catechism. Going to the mountains away from the house and chores was peaceful and quiet. It was also enjoyable. No one knew about this except for Mom's closest relatives. We couldn't go to church because there was no church. The church was too far. We had a picnic instead. During Lent and Holy Week we abstained from eating the first meal of the day. We traveled on foot to the cemeteries as penance to pray. We visited the graves of loved ones and took saints with us. We knelt on the earth and kissed the earth.

We ate special foods such as *panocha*, sprouted wheat with no yeast, *sopa* bread, Lenten food, and sweet rice during Holy Week. *Buñuelos* were eaten during Lent, during Christmas and special occasions. It was a fried pastry.

We buried our dead the next day. Everyone in the village was notified, and the whole night was spent in prayer and song. We would sit in the house. Relatives may have stayed a week. Everybody brought food and we mourned for one year. We covered the doors and mirrors with a black cloth. Nickels were placed under the eyelids of the deceased until the person went cold. Otherwise the dead person would have open eyes. Nickels were used to close the eyelids.

Older women were very secretive from children, especially girls. They didn't want them to be familiar with the sexual aspect of life. Boys and girls were baptized about a week or two after birth. Slitting their throats with one quick move killed animals. They were hung to drain the blood. We didn't eat blood. We didn't eat eggs with blood spots.

When asked why I was named Cecilia, Mom said that Grandfather was named Cecilio and wanted his name used. In Spanish culture, a child is named for the living and the dead. Mother had a man make a tombstone for Great-Grandfather on her father's side. He carved a dove on it. Great-Grandmother made butter and stamped the butter with what looked like wheat with eight points.

I suspect that I have this heritage because I have a long genealogical lineage to Spain and Mexico. I'm almost eighty years old. I'm sure that I have Indian and Jewish blood.

## Charles M. Carrillo

My name is Charles M. Carrillo. I was born in Albuquerque, New Mexico, in 1956. By the time I was five or six years old I was aware of my Jewish ancestry because of the family talk. We always joked about my nose; the family said my nose was shaped a certain way because of my Jewish ancestry. As it happens, my great-great-grandmother was an Espinosa, a Sephardic Spanish family who were *conversos*. We never spoke about this. However, we maintained rituals that we never knew were Jewish, such as placing stones on fresh graves, etc. I am told that some of my ancestors even lit candles on Friday evenings.

As I grew into adulthood, I joined the Penitente Brotherhood who always pray for the departed souls with a traditional prayer called *El Sudario*. We are keenly aware of our Jewish ancestry. However, being so Roman Catholic, we have almost completely forgotten why we do so many of the rituals

## Consuelo (Connie) Jaramillo Delgado

I know there is Judaism on the Jaramillo side, my paternal side. My paternal grandmother was on the Espinoza side.

I never knew anything as a kid. I read a lot as a child and couldn't watch TV. I read World War II books and read *Exodus*. I had an affinity for reading about Israel. In fact, I told my sisters that I would join the Israeli Air Force. I read about the *Masad*, the Israeli police, and how they would bring people to Israel and try them. When I read *Exodus* there was a girl named Aliyah. My sister and I said we would name our children Aliyah. My sister used that name for her daughter.

We visited our Espinoza grandmother often growing up. About five years ago, I read an article in *La Herencia* about *conversos*. I told Dad that our last name was on the list of names Jews took when they left Spain. Espinoza was also on that list. Jaramillo is a place where certain plants grow. *Espina* are like spiny sticker plants. Espinoza might come from *espina*, things of nature.

I remember Dad telling me about playing with a dreidel, *pon y saca*. A couple of years ago we had a dreidel for Christmas. He told me things were done on the Espinoza side. I told him that if he doesn't share it, "It will die with you."

Grandmother Espinoza lit candles on Friday night. Candles were lit in a *nicho* (hole in the wall). Their *Sabbath* was Saturday. They did the bare minimum of work on Saturday. Dad's grandfather wouldn't go to church and read the Bible at home. They didn't go to church on Sunday.

Grandfather told Father's mother (Espinoza) that they were different. He never told them that they were Jews. There is a Pedro Jaramillo who came with Oñate. It was always instilled in us that we came from Spain. My parents were adamant that "we're Spanish and not Mexicans." Everyone who came to the New World went through Mexico. *Conversos* came to escape the Inquisition and signed on for expeditions. There was a *mezuzah* (recognized now) up on the rafter of Grandmother Espinoza's house so that it would be hidden. Dad is the oldest of ten kids. Dad's sister, the younger of twins, remembers it.

They covered mirrors and buried the dead quickly. When Father's own grandfather died, he remembers covering the mirrors. They had a *Luto* where mourners sit in the house and sing *alabados*, mournful songs in Spanish. I don't know how long this was, but people visited and brought food. We lit candles on the one-year anniversary of a loved-one's death in our own house. They would say, "I do my own praying here (in the house)." Part of the family who practiced Catholicism said a mass in church on the year anniversary of the death.

The history of the church in New Mexico included traveling priests. In the 1800s *morada*s were frowned upon by the church. A lot of people wouldn't go to church. They had to pay for a pew. Grandfather on Mom's side, Quintana, wouldn't pay and wouldn't go to church. He read the Bible at home.

Dad's father's name was Solomon Jaramillo. Names in the family are Paul, Reuben, Joseph, and Rebecca. They are Dad's siblings.

When I was a kid, my sisters called me "Jewish Mama" because I said I will join the Israeli Air Force. We would pretend we were on a *kibbutz*.

Dad said the family only slaughtered animals amongst themselves. They sliced the neck a certain way and never ate blood. They let the blood drain and salted the meat.

During Lent, we ate *panocha*. *Torta de huevo* was eaten during Lent. It was an egg dish with red chili and no meat. We ate rice pudding, *capirotada*, which was similar to *panocha* (raisins and cheese). *Quelites* were eaten during Lent.

We did a play about Mary and Joseph looking for a place for Jesús to be born. There was a play each night along with bonfires. These plays were called *Posadas* and were done nine nights before Christmas and were supposed to light the way of Mary and Joseph to Bethlehem. We celebrated *Mis Christmas*. Kids would go around from house to house during *Posadas* (nine days). They would usually go to relatives or close-knit neighbors and get money or fruit. This was common up to Mom's generation. They did *Las Posadas* within the church.

Dad remembers he knew different words in Spanish than people spoke. His grandfather spoke a different Spanish.

When visiting the grave of a loved one, Dad's side placed stones on the headstones. People who were *conversos* would put a fence around their burial plot. We believed in circumcision, early in life, soon after birth. Women covered their heads with a *mantilla* in church. They did this back then. In the Bernalillo church, you see a couple of older ladies do it.

Education was very important. Dad was sent to boarding school in the sixth grade. He graduated high school in the normal school. I have seven sisters (eight children) and all went through college. *Empanadas* were filled with fruit (apple, pumpkin, raisins) or meat.

Our people married within their own up to my father's generation. Second or third cousins married. We ate pork but didn't raise pigs. Dad said people had to survive. A majority of the time we ate beef, lamb, and chicken. We killed the chicken by twirling it to break its neck. Mom stayed in the house forty days after birth. You didn't leave and didn't attend church. Mom and Grandmother said not to wet hair so we wouldn't catch cold. When we went swimming we were told to do this.

My parents and I grew up in Las Cruces. Dad carried on from his parents. We would kneel down and receive a blessing when we were ready to leave.

Mom would make the sign of the cross with salt if there was a bad rainstorm with lightning.

We had icons in our home. We ate *pan de semita*. I don't know when it was eaten, but Mom said her mom made it.

Grandmother set aside a piece of dough when baking bread. I think Judaism is my culture, and it's part of us and important for us to know more about it. Dad, when asked, says it's in the past.

I'd probably never convert, but feel a strong affinity to anything Jewish and support Israel. I wore a Star of David in high school.

## Consuelo Luz Arostegui

Consuelo Luz Paz de la Gloria Caterina Arostegui Dávila is my full name. I was baptized on "Saturday of Glory," thus the "de la Gloria." This was a common way that *converso* (or hidden) Jews referred to Saturday as a special day without making reference to the *Sabbath.* I took Caterina as a confirmation name after one of my favorite Catholic saints and a nun I adored at Maryknoll School in Rome. Luz is my aunt's name and Paz is my mother's name. Arostegui is my father's Basque family name (my father was Cuban) and Dávila is my mother's family name (from Chile).

Throughout my childhood I remember hearing references to our "Jewish ancestry." Most particularly, I recall hearing that we were related to Saint Teresa of Ávila on my mother's side of the family (Dávila meaning from Ávila). This made a huge impression on me, especially since I was being raised Catholic by a Colombian nanny, and I resolved to become a saint when I grew up.

My parents did not practice any religion, never went to church, and seemed puzzled by my devout Catholicism. I prayed that God would forgive them for not believing in the Resurrection and they would go to heaven anyway. My nanny tells me the pope in Rome confirmed me, but I don't remember because I was delirious with fever that day.

I settled in northern New Mexico in my early twenties and married a Jewish man. My now ex-husband took me to my first *Yom Kippur* service and I was entranced and moved deeply by the spiritual connection I felt to this special day.

Around that time, the New Mexican state historian had started sharing his findings from his research on the Jewish ancestry of many of the New Mexico Hispanic families. Rabbi Chavah Carp of Taos showed me some religious songs in a language called Ladino (very similar to the ancient Spanish spoken in the villages of northern New Mexico) and asked me to learn some of them to sing at services. These haunting, passionate songs spoke to something very deep in me and inspired me to write a special song for my son, Max, to sing on his *bar mitzvah*.

I started inquiring among family members about our Jewish ancestry. My mother, Paz Dávila de Arostegui, who lives in Spain, told me she believed the strongest Jewish connection was on her father's mother's Espinoza side (related to the famed Jewish philosopher Spinoza). My aunt,

Luz Dávila de Carrasco, who lives in Chile, told me the following story:

When my Grandfather Carlos Dávila Espinoza was dying of cancer in Washington, D.C., in the mid- 1950s, his nephew, Dr. Miguel Millán, traveled to Washington from Chile to care for him. My grandfather was secretary general of the Organization of American States at the time. He had been a founder of the OAS, of the United Nations, and in 1932 he was also the leader of the first socialist revolution in the Western Hemisphere, in Chile, which lasted for a few short months during which he served as president of Chile—before going into exile under threats of assassination.

Before my cousin Miguel died in the late 1990s, he confided to my aunt that Carlos, on his deathbed, had told Miguel, *"Somos Judíos"* (we are Jews). Miguel had waited until he was dying, almost fifty years later, to pass this on to another member of the family.

My grandfather had lost his first wife, my Grandmother Herminia, to cancer when she was in her early forties. Herminia Arrate de Dávila was a respected artist in Chile and a beloved hostess in Washington, D.C., where my grandfather was ambassador from 1927 to 1931. Later, President Franklin D. Roosevelt, being very fond of my grandparents, was to order that Air Force One be used to transport my grandmother back to Chile so she could die in her native land surrounded by her family.

Carlos married Frances Adams, a direct descendant of President John Adams, many years later. In the last several years, I have had many wonderful conversations with my step-grandmother, Frances. Among her many delightful stories, she informed me that Carlos told her that Herminia's great-great-grandfather had been a rabbi.

As I researched deeper into my Sephardic background, I continued singing the Sephardic songs I discovered in Taos.

I sing at High Holy Days in the Temple Beth Shalom in Santa Fe, *bar mitzvahs*, weddings, special services, and internationally, at venues such as the Sephardic Arts Festival in Los Angeles, Les Orientales Sacred Music Festival in France, the World Expo in Germany, the U.S. Southwest Jewish Cantors' Conference in Santa Fe, and the Jewish Community Center in Havana, Cuba. I recently released a CD of these songs titled DEZEO (www.consueloluz.com).

I feel this music came to me as a gift and as a holy task, and it is my sacred responsibility to share the spiritual power and beauty of these songs with as many people as possible. The spiritual energy released by these long-hidden songs is cherished by the congregation in Santa Fe. I hope to spread the singing of these songs and their Sephardic spirit to Jewish congregations across the country and also, as "world music," use these songs to bring together people from all cultures and beliefs in the loving and joyous celebration of our universal soul.

## David López

I know we're Jewish just by the fact that we came from Spain. My aunt said we were of Jewish descent from Spain. The family came in the 1600s through the Caribbean, to Mexico, and up the Rio Grande to Santa Fe.

I consider myself Jewish because I have a business and try to be self-employed and independent. Some names in the family are López, Leyba, Cruz, and Vialpando. Our grandparents blessed us by making a cross on our foreheads.

After burial, we would throw handfuls of dirt on the coffin.

When I go to see Mom's or Dad's grave, I say a prayer. There used to be a one-year mourning period. In the forties, fifties, and sixties people dressed in black for the one year, and the women didn't go to church without a veil.

I'm not involved in the church. My grandparents were Catholic and went to church. There were icons in the house, and they were not secretive. They had a miniature cathedral in a back room and prayed in that dark room without windows.

Many people told us that our Spanish in northern New Mexico was a different dialect.

We killed animals with a rifle or an ax. Chickens were twirled until they were decapitated. We never drank blood but rather drained the blood of animals. We did cook the blood of a pig.

Our *Sabbath* was on Sunday. During Holy Week or Lent we didn't eat meat. We didn't chew gum. There was no work whatsoever. At this time, we ate *panocha*, eggs, and *capirotada*. *Quelites* are eaten in the spring when they are really fresh.

During Christmas, we ate *buñuelos*. We had a *Mis Christmas* where the children went from house to house on Christmas morning and were given candy, coins, oranges, and fruit.

There was no circumcision. After birth, the women stayed in the house more than a month. We would throw salt up and with a knife, cut the sky to stop the rain. I love our Jewish heritage, and the family feels the same.

**Delia Abreu Casaus**

Abreu is Spanish, not a Portuguese name. My ancestors, on Father's side, came from Cadiz, Spain, and the name, Abreu, first appeared here in 1795. The first Abreu was Santiago Abreu. His son, Jesús, is my great-grandfather. Ramón Abreu was my father.

On Father's side, my aunts said that Grandfather told them that our ancestor came from Cadiz, Spain. Their grandfather, Santiago, died in 1837 and was killed by the Indians. My grandfather, Jesús (son of Santiago) was born in 1823.

They slaughtered the animals by slitting their throats and shooting them. Then they were hung to drain the blood. I saw mother twirl chickens to kill them. It took about two twirls. It was very fast. Then she cut their heads off.

We ate *panocha* during Lent because we were not supposed to eat meat. *Panocha* is sprouted wheat, and it is sweetened. It is made into a pudding.

*Empanadas* were eaten during Christmas and Easter. *Capirotada* was eaten at any time. It's made with cheese, raisins, cinnamon, butter, and bread.

We owned a chapel at the ranch, and it still belongs to the family. We went into the chapel with a shawl or a hat on our heads. All women kept their heads covered. This is not done anymore.

We ate *quelites*, greens that grew wild. We ate these whenever we could get them. They came out in the summer.

Father was buried the next day. People visited for one day after the burial. My father died when I was thirteen years old. We mourned or wore black for a year a few generations back. People visited after the funeral for two or three days.

We ate *buñuelos* whenever we made bread. We put them in hot fat and they blew up. The whole outside was crispy, and it was hollow inside.

I can't think of anything, although my aunts were very religious. They went to church every morning. I never heard anything or saw anything. If I thought I had this heritage, I would tell you.

**Delores Nancy Ramona Montoya Montoya Esquibel**

The first Montoya is Dad's name from a place bordering Colorado and New Mexico. The second Montoya is Mom's name from New Mexico. Great-Grandfather Juan Casías, on Dad's side, married an Indian woman from Taos, New Mexico. I don't know how many children he had. Great-Grandfather had a child out of wedlock. Great-Grandmother raised this child. She inherited the ranch.

The ranch was like a little community where people had names such as Trujillo, Durán, and Casías. All were related. Generally, cousins married cousins, up to the third cousin. Some married first cousins.

Grandmother Molly, Mother's mother, raised me. Molly had some German Jewish heritage. Her father, Félix Martín, was a German Jew. During World War I, Félix Martín was called back to Germany. He wanted to take his family, but Grandmother Rita, Molly's mother, wouldn't go. He never came back. Rita was very secretive, and I was raised with the Spanish influence.

Molly married Grandfather Ventura who was a Montoya. His great-grandfather was Agapito Montoya. Agapito and his wife lived in Santa Cruz, New Mexico. They raised two sons and two daughters. Agapito's sons were Martín and Ted Montoya. Mother is from Agapito's lineage. Almost everyone in this valley is related. Martín Montoya was my great-grandfather. The family goes back to Spain and may have been one of the first to settle here. They were told Agapito's grandfather came from Spain. The Queen of Spain sent him to New Mexico. He was not allowed to practice his religion and had to be Catholic. The family, Agapito's lineage, said they left Spain because they weren't wanted there. That's why I think most Spanish here are Jewish. They were made to change their last names. The ancestors came from Spain and were Basque.

The real old homes had thick walls and they could put secret things between the walls. Agapito's home had three fireplaces. During the Pueblo revolt, Agapito hid in the fireplaces. That saved him. They hid objects in the walls. The family never said anything. Even now, some members of the family are secretive. They don't want others to know anything. The relatives looked European.

Grandfather was the boss. Religious things were influenced by Grandfather. He was a Penitente. He told us we had to go to church. He was born in 1899 but never said where he was born. Agapito was born in the 1700s.

Ventura, my grandfather, would go to the *morada*. I went with him. They went in the back. They had a little kitchen separate from the *morada* for the women to cook for the men. They did these things secretly. There weren't any windows. They prayed on Friday night in the *morada* and spent the night there. Ventura went into a back room to pray. As a child it was spooky to me. The windows were covered in the whole house. The windows were small.

During Lent, all these men would go in the dark to the *morada*. They were from Santa Cruz. My son went in once, and they would do chanting and turn on candles in the dark.

We ate pork on the ranch in Santa Cruz. I noticed my Spanish was different. I asked the priest. He said, "Don't worry. Your Spanish is right. I come from Spain and mine is right to me."

My Grandmother Molly said you had to go to Catholic school no matter what. Most of the time, nuns were nice. I couldn't speak Spanish in Catholic schools. I light my important candles on Friday night. Ventura raised me. We didn't do anything on the weekend and rested on Saturday and Sunday. We didn't work on either day and cleaned the house on Friday. I knew *Sabbath* was Saturday from Grandfather Ventura and Mother, his daughter. The whole community knew this. Ventura said there is only one God who takes care of everyone. Ventura never talked and would visit his family alone.

The family believed in circumcision, including Dad. Most Catholics here do. We'd baptize children a week after birth. Most of us did, and we had a celebration.

If someone died, we brought the deceased home. Afterward people brought food. Coins were placed on the eyes to close them. During the burial, people threw handfuls of dirt into the grave. This is still done. The family used to fill up the grave, but now it's done by the cemetery workers. Mourning was for one year.

Growing up, the villagers observed *Sabbath* on Saturday and Sunday. Grandmother said Saturday was the *Sabbath* because it was the day Jesús rested. Catholics celebrate Sunday.

In New Mexico, people painted all windows and doors blue to keep evil spirits out. Everyone in the family sweeps to the center of the room. This is still done. That's how I did it at home.

The family killed sheep by cutting the throat with a special knife. It was hung by its hind legs, and the blood was drained into a hole in the earth. Ventura covered it with dirt, and we didn't eat the blood. Eggs with blood spots were thrown out. My daughters still do it. We salt meat and don't eat a lot of pork. We killed the chicken by twirling it until it was decapitated and drained the blood.

My sons, daughters, and myself are lactose intolerant. We stayed in the house six weeks after birth. My daughters didn't do it. The family would bless you by placing both hands on the head and then making the sign of the cross. People around here did it. My parents would put water on my head before we went to the Catholic Church. They would spray a little holy water and say, "We baptize you in the name of the Father, the Son, and the Holy Spirit." This was done to all the children. Grandfather Ventura did it. They said these things were tradition. That's what we do in our family. This is not done now, that I know of. Maybe it's still done in the hill towns where it is more isolated. I heard that it's done in those places, but the people don't talk to you. I feel I'm Jewish. I don't know what to do. I'm between two worlds. You're split.

During Lent, we had unleavened bread in the Catholic Church. They give a host that is unleavened bread. Sisters did this and gave unleavened bread at anytime during the year, but it was more important during Lent. The only time we ate *panocha* was during Lent.

We ate *buñuelos*, *sopapillas*, and *empanaditas* (with prunes and raisins) on special occasions such as Christmas and New Year's. We would make them on these special occasions. We would buy those we ate at other times. We played with a top during Christmas. Most of the neighbors were secretive and wouldn't talk about what went on in the house.

Grandmother and Grandfather stressed the Old Testament. They talked more about the Old Testament than the New Testament. I believe I have Jewish blood. I went to synagogue once and was not comfortable. None of my brothers and sisters are interested. I practiced the rituals with my grandparents.

### Dora Chávez Durán

My name is Dora Chávez Durán. Mother's name is Mondragón, from the Vigil side. Dad was Chávez. We know that Dad's great-grandfather said they came from Mexico and went up to Colorado. Then they went back down to Los Hueros, New Mexico. Grandfather built a Catholic Church in Los Hueros, and it was called Los Hueros because they were blond and blue-eyed from Spain. *Hueros* means blond. The mother of my cousin, on Dad's side, said that our ancestors came from Spain. I'm sure they came for a better life, but I don't know why they came. Dad's first cousin said that on the family tree, Dad's family is linked back to Cortéz.

We grew up in a small village, Naranjos, New Mexico. We were told that we spoke an archaic form of Spanish. Ester is a biblical name in the family. My mother's sister is Ester. When Mom's dad died, there was a twenty-four hour burial. People visited and brought food for a few days after the burial. I thought it was because they couldn't go home right away. It wasn't fast and easy to travel, the way it is today. We observed a one-year mourning period, with the wearing of black. Mother lit candles on the year anniversary of the deceased. They still light candles and offer a special mass on the year anniversary of someone's death. When someone died, coins were placed over the eyes of the deceased. My mother covered the mirrors, but I don't remember when or why. She did this after someone died and during other times of the year, some ritualistic times. When I got older, she stopped.

We would sweep away from the door. When killing sheep, Dad drained the blood. He also twirled the chicken until it was decapitated. Meat was salted. Eggs with blood spots were thrown out. After the birth of a child, the woman would stay in bed for ten days without bathing. She would stay in the house for forty days. Everyone around here does the forty days. She was told not to look in the mirror, not to look at the moon, and not to eat pork. Grandmother delivered the children. Father buried the placenta and then slaughtered a sheep.

Women would cover their heads when they went to church. My mother and sister do this. Dad never told us anything. When asked, he said, "Mind your own business." Then he changed the subject.

During Holy Week, before Easter, we ate *panocha*s, made with sprouted wheat that didn't rise. We didn't eat meat but ate fish. We ate *torta de huevo*, made from eggs and flour. It was fried and mixed with chili. This was unleavened bread that was also eaten when we were not allowed to eat meat. We ate *empanadas* during March. They were filled with pumpkin fruit. *Buñuelos* were eaten during Christmas and were fried.

We made pork and beans without cheese. Usually it was made with cheese, but I didn't know this. As for any connection to Judaism, it is fine. I feel comfortable with it.

**Dora Marina Roe**

I didn't know that I had this heritage. I was twenty-one when my mother sat me down and said, "I have something I need to tell you." She said my father, Henry, was not my real father. "Your real father, Rodolfo Morales, wants to see you.

That's why I'm telling you this. He never wanted to stop being part of your life. I've kept him from you all these years because I was afraid that you would feel a separation from your half sisters (Henry's and Mom's children)." We were united into one happy family. It didn't surprise me. Since I was a little girl, I dreamed I was adopted. I didn't know in my dream if my mom, dad, or both knew there was someone else somewhere. I was surprised because that was the solution to the puzzle.

Everywhere I went I was told that I looked different than my sisters. Mother said that she had seen a picture of my paternal grandmother, and I looked like her. Then she said one other thing, "Your father is Jewish." I know (through Mom) that my grandmother died giving birth to my real father. When I've completed school, studying for a nursing degree, I will research the family history.

I went to see Father twice. It was important to me and to him that I know where I came from. He told me that he had never stopped looking for me. My mother turned him away. When I was twenty-one, he knew she could no longer legally stop him.

My father said that my paternal grandmother (I don't know her name) was from Spain where she met my paternal grandfather. She was an Orthodox Jew, and her parents disowned her for marrying my paternal grandfather who was a traveling bullfighter, fighting in Spain at the time. He was born in Guadalajara, Mexico, and traveled to Spain. After they married, they moved to Guadalajara.

On Father's line, Grandfather's name was Rodolfo Pulido (bullfighter). Pulido means to polish. This may have Jewish origins. Mom is Hispanic and her name was Rivera. She was born in Chihuahua, Mexico, as well as my maternal grandmother, Marina Natalia Rivera. Mother's father was Rosendo Peres. He never said his family was from Spain. On Mom's side, I know she has a sister in Guadalajara and was raised within the Hispanic culture. Father was adopted by a childless couple because Grandfather's work took him away. He was born in Guadalajara, Mexico. I don't know when they came to Guadalajara. I know my paternal grandparents met in Spain.

My great-grandmother on my mother's side was Elijia Rivera. My maternal grandmother, Natalia Rivera, was raised Catholic. Yet, she named my mother Dora. You were supposed to name your children after a Catholic saint. The Catholic midwife asked, "What are you going to name the child?" Grandmother said, "Dora." The midwife said, "The name Dora is not a saint's name." My grandmother asked the midwife, "What name can I give her that is a saint's name?" On the midwife's suggestion, she named her Clara but kept Dora as the first name. Grandmother said, "Then it will be Dora Clara." My grandmother never called her Clara, and my mother never used that name. My grandmother was raised Catholic, and as a Catholic, it was surprising that she had no idea that Dora wasn't a saint's name. In the Catholic Church a child is named after a saint. You can give them as many names as you want, but one of the names has to be after a saint. Dorit is my Hebrew name, and it means generation.

My maternal grandmother could not pray without lighting candles and always covered her head to pray. She did this every evening. Mom's family wouldn't talk about the past. You never looked at them or any older person (parents, grandparents) in the eye when they were giving you a lecture. It was like you were disrespecting them or giving them the evil eye. They would say, "You're going to give me the evil eye." You were to sit there with your head down. Mother's mother hates Christmas—detests it. She was raised this way. She once mentioned that relatives may have come from Spain because of their light skin. The Riveras look like Anglos, some red-headed with green and blue eyes, white skin and freckles.

Mom said there were a lot of secrets in the family, and

they didn't want to talk about it. My mother, when she was fifteen, went to confession and the priest made a pass at her. She never went back. She changed to the Baptist Church. I was raised that way even though I was baptized in the Catholic Church. My mother was seventeen when I was born. Her mother was still Catholic. To this day, Mom is a Baptist and hates Christmas. She hates Easter, all the fuss. My mother will get up in an ugly mood during these holidays.

I spent my formative years in New Mexico. Mother was from Chihuahua and was told her Spanish was different than in New Mexico because they spoke Ladino. I realized they spoke Ladino when I read about it. The Riveras speak Ladino. We didn't have icons in our home. Mom hated saints. Grandmother had saint figurines that candles were on. I don't remember icons in Grandmother's house.

We would come home from school on Fridays and make sure everything was clean for the weekend, Saturday and Sunday. My mother or grandmother never swept dirt past the doorway. I got in big trouble when they saw me doing it. They said it was not correct to do it.

My grandmother had a little thing by the door with holy water. She would dip her hand in the water and cross herself when entering and leaving the house. Mom was very strict that we did not worship saints. "You don't pray to saints. You don't look at them. When you pray, you bow your head and pray." Mom said, "There is no Virgin Mary. We do not worship Mary as far as her being the mother of Jesús. She is simply remembered as the tool God used to bring Jesús into the world, but we do not put her on a pedestal." Mom is Christian, but is not convinced about the different beliefs within the religion.

My grandmother and mother would cook meat until it was well-done and didn't have blood. We ate pork, but this was rarely done. My step-grandfather took a chicken and twirled it until it was decapitated. It was hung to drain the blood. Mom was raised by her mother Natalia and step-grandfather. They drained the blood and would dig a hole and bury it. Mom wouldn't use eggs with blood spots. We never ate anything with blood. Everything was cooked completely. Mother took all fat and veins from the meat. We would not drink milk and watermelon together.

My little brother was circumcised. Mother's brother is David. I would hear Grandmother say that it has been a year since so and so died, and then she went to her candles and lit them. She didn't go to church to do it, only at home.

We didn't observe Lent. I never remember my mother or grandmother saying, "Don't eat meat because it is Friday." Grandmother and Mom made *buñuelos* around New Year's. When someone was leaving or going on a trip, Grandmother would put one hand on their shoulder and make the sign of the cross. We said grace after meals, thanking God for the food. My maternal grandmother would put a piece of bread in a jar in the cabinet so there would always be bread in the house. I have a jar with bread so we'll always have bread. We wouldn't throw salt away because we were concerned about not having any more. Salt was like the spice of life.

My grandmother was not able to go to school. My mother has a bachelor's degree. I'm working on mine. Once, after she finished talking to an uncle, Grandmother Natalia dipped her hand in the holy water on the door and sprinkled it on him. I never remember Grandmother telling anyone to go to confession.

With children, a lot of times a child would get sick and they didn't know where the illness was coming from. Grandmother Rivera would rub a raw egg in the shell on the child's body to ward off the evil eye. Prayers were said during this cleaning (*limpia*). In effect, you were cleansing the body of the evil eye. After you were done, if the egg had a blood spot, they would say it was the evil eye. She was also a midwife.

I returned to Judaism, and the children did too. Mom didn't, and she's fine with it. I hated going through conversion because I felt that I was always Jewish. I never could swallow church doctrine. I always asked questions. As a result, in Sunday school of the Baptist Church, teachers would tell me to go home and ask Jesús to come into my heart and that He would help me to understand.

Judaism makes a lot more sense to me. I believe my thinking has always been Jewish. I'm not a person that conforms to whatever. I always ask questions. If someone asks, "Why did you return," I say, "Why not?" Mom said, "You can never go by the rules. Your father had a very stubborn nature, and you're exactly like him." She said, "You were never around your father and you are just like him." I was very athletic and so was my father. My daughter has Hirschsprung, a rare congenital disease which is common in Jewish people. This disease is where cells in the large intestine that squeeze food down through the canal are missing. She had corrective surgery. I still have many questions about where I came from because I have many relatives out there, and I would like to find them. I am the first in my family to be born in this country, on both sides.

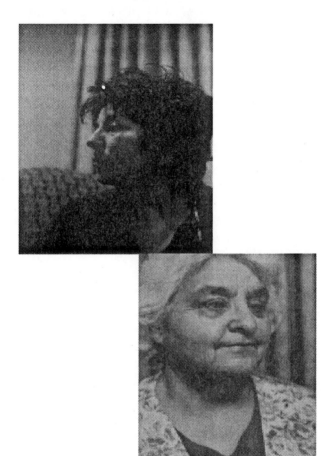

**Emilia Vigil and Betty Sandoval (Sisters)**

**Betty**

The names on Father's side are Leyba and Pacheco. On Mother's side the names are Vásquez and Romero. Some relatives spelled Vásquez with a B, as in Básquez.

The family didn't mix well with others, only with the Presbyterian Community. We were raised as Presbyterians. As we grew up, we hung around together because we were Jews who were forced to convert. We were the same people with the same heritage. Most people were related and helped each other. When we went to Wyoming, we kept to ourselves. They were such a mixture of people.

We came back to northern New Mexico, and I didn't fit with the people and the church. I felt that I didn't belong. I said, "Lord, take away the mask and tell me who I am." I didn't belong and wanted to find my roots. The Lord spoke to me and said, "You're Jews." I started looking at Jews, and they were so similar. However, I felt we needed proof.

My sister, Christina, went to Laramie, Wyoming, and pried the information out of Uncle Secundino. She said, "Uncle, what are our roots?" Finally, he said, "Daughter, *hijita*, our family were Jews, and we were put on boats like sheep, in Spain, and put to sea." It was not talked about in the family. Uncle Secundino was Grandmother's cousin, but everyone called him Uncle. My family, on the Vásquez side, said they originally came from Spain.

### Emilia

My grandmother (Dad's mother) always called my mother Isha. It means woman. This name is found in the King James Bible, in the Old Testament. At home we were raised reading the Bible. My sister, Christina, met a Jewish woman from the Basque region of Spain who told her that Isha meant woman. She also said Leyba means Lion.

### Betty

We were told that our Spanish is a little different, sixteenth century Spanish. Ladino is Spanish with Hebrew words. We said grace before and after meals. I've never lost it and have always done it. My kids do it too. This is a Jewish custom.

We sweep to the middle of the room. Mom covered the mirrors when someone died and turned pictures to the wall.

During Christmas, we did not give gifts in our family. The teachers at the Presbyterian Mission School would give a small gift such as a coloring book, but we didn't give gifts within the family. We ate *buñuelos*. They are deep-fried pastries that were eaten at Christmas and other times.

We didn't eat many foods. We ate more vegetables than meat. We didn't eat shellfish. The only fish we ate was trout. We mainly ate fish, turkey, and venison. Sometimes, people gave us pork, but we didn't raise pigs. Dad's family didn't raise pigs. Their meat was beef or chicken. On Mom's side, they raised sheep and goats.

Animals were killed with a sharpened knife and the jugular was cut. We hanged a cow, for instance, by the hind legs to drain the blood. They salted the meat and hung it to dry. A cow would be slaughtered in late September or October. It would then be cut into pieces and hung to drain in the cellar. In the winter it was cold, and so the meat would freeze and drain, freeze and drain. It just drained, and this is still done today. We would slice it when it was partially frozen. It would slice real thin and then they would salt it. It was again hung to dry and made into a beef jerky or dried meat. Before we ate it, Mom would run it through the hot oven so it wasn't raw. To this day, I don't like blood in meat.

Mom's brother made tops. When I went to a Sephardic meeting, I found out they were called dreidels. They weren't round. Around it there were letters. When women had babies, they stayed in bed for forty days.

The family converted to Presbyterianism before Mom was born. When the missionaries went into the valley of Chacón, in northern New Mexico, people joined the Presbyterian Church. Grandma hated crosses. We came from Pecos to Chacón. Grandfather's father helped Mother's side build a church in Chacón. The whole family went to the Presbyterian Church. It didn't have any icons. The only thing in the church was scripture from the King James Old Testament: "But the Lord is in His holy temple. Let all the earth keep silent before Him." The *Tanakh* is the Hebrew Old Testament. Here it said, "But *Ha-Shem* is in His holy sanctuary. Let all the world be silent before Him." My father's side was Catholic.

Mom remembers the mountain in Chacón where we lived. It had a cabin with one window, and that window was covered with a quilt. The men went into the cabin on Friday night with shawls. They would close the door. Mom didn't know why they did this. They probably wore prayer shawls. Mom was a little girl at the time.

Families married within their particular community and stayed together in the same area. The people would call each other cousins. We would cover mirrors in New Mexico when people died. The wake was for one night followed by a twenty-four hour burial. Neighbors would bring food the day of the funeral. We had a one-year mourning period and the women wore black. We are both Messianic now. We have a community *Shabbat* once a month with mainstream Judaism.

### Betty

I feel a connection to Judaism. I feel like I came home and didn't have to search anymore.

### Emilia

I accepted Judaism—no struggle.

## Father Symeon Clemente Carmona

I realized my heritage in my pre-teens. The incident, in which I found out, took place by having an argument or fight with other kids in which we were called strange names. Coming home and telling my mother of it, she told me to go to my great-grandfather and tell him exactly what had happened.

My grandfather took me out to sit beneath a large cottonwood tree that grew in the yard. He proceeded to speak of the Old Testament and the Jewish people. As he spoke, I interrupted him, and I asked, "What does that have to do with us?" It took a few seconds, and he answered me, hugging me at the same time, "But, my child, we are the people in the Old Testament. We are Jewish. You are a Jew." And he continued on for an hour or two, telling the history of the family, who we were and how we came to be in this place, New Mexico.

In our home, for instance, all the men ate together from the youngest male to the oldest male; and then the females ate, after the men would eat. The mother, in whose home the dinner was served, always served the first-born male first and then the other males. Before eating the meal, the oldest male in the house would bless bread with a special prayer and bless a glass of wine of which everybody at the table partook a little. We were taught, for instance, to recite the psalms in Latin, usually done by the first-born son who was made to study different languages from his very earliest years, such as Spanish, Ladino, English, Latin, and a little bit of Hebrew. One of the interesting parts in this was that he was taught to recite everything from memory so as to not leave any incriminating evidence to the church. Other things remembered as a ritual that the women did: At the beginning of every month they would symbolically wash their hands in a bowl of water that was placed at the so-called family altar and dry their hands with green grass or leaves. They would drop a silver coin into the water and leave it there. I finally realized that this was a woman's purification ritual and the coins represented the coin given to the priest after the purification. The purification was for the monthly menstrual cycle.

Yes, I feel connected to Judaism and the Jewish people in a great way, first, realizing that the faith I now hold came from the Jewish people, that it has the same ritual laws, rules, and regulations. Also, now that I am a priest monk, members of the *Marrano* community come to me to seek counsel about whether to return to Judaism fully or remain, as we are, a dying dinosaur in this place and time. They bring their children sometimes for me to bless them in the Jewish way, by laying of hands and reciting Ladino prayers over them. I believe that I am one of the very few persons in this world that can come through the door of time, and on either side, will be my family, my people, my joy, my all.

## Felicitas Gloria Armijo

My father was Cayetano Torres. My mother's name was Adela Holguín. The H was dropped.

Father said that we had origins from Spain. Father and an uncle spoke of our family being here for about five hundred years. We have traced Holguín to records in Spain. Juan López Holguín, native of Fuente Ovejuna in Estremadura, Spain, son of Juan López Villasana, came to Mexico and then to New Mexico with Oñate in 1600 and brought along his wife. In 1626, Juan López Holguín gave his age as sixty-four saying that he was a "founder of the kingdom of Nueva España." Among the Torres people living in New Mexico when the Indians rebelled in 1680, was Cristóbal de Torres I who was not yet traced back to Spain. His son, Cristóbal Torres II, was a native of New Mexico. Cristóbal Torres II was a soldier and married at Guadalupe del Paso in 1698, but by 1710 he was in Albuquerque. Torres folk appear in the Oñate list of 1597. Some of these Torreses were wagon train masters. Cristóbal

Torres II was given a large land grant near the old pueblo of Chama, in the northwest part of New Mexico. Cristóbal II's son, Diego de Torres, was given the Belen land grant in 1740.

We were merchants. People felt we must be Jews from Mexico because we were merchants. Jews were traders, and it was assumed we were Mexican Jews because we started our own business. Being called a "Mexican Jew" was derogatory in those days. To me, being called a "Mexican Jew" was always derogatory.

When we were growing up, Dad was teaching us math. I didn't understand. We were living near pueblos and with Indians. When I couldn't grasp a problem, Dad would say, negatively, "Well, you're Indian." He knew my mom was of Indian ancestry. Some of our origins were Indian. We can't say what tribe because these Indians were displaced people that had lost their identity. They were placed in the Spanish homes, not as slaves, but as domestics. They melted into the pot, took Spanish names, their ways and speech.

I was told that the Torres family came from Sevilla, Spain. When Oñate was coming along the Camino Real from Mexico in 1598, he named the present-day La Joya Nueva Sevilla; it reminded him of Sevilla, Spain. These towns were *parajes* (resting places). All towns were resting places or stopping places. The Indians prevented the permanent establishment of communities. When it became safe to live there, settlements were formed and groups of families came.

In public school, we were led to believe we came with the Pilgrims on the Mayflower. We heard of the Penitentes but never participated. Most everyone was devoutly Catholic. We had *santos* in our home and church. My parents and grandparents grew up in Belen, New Mexico.

When we moved south of Socorro in 1939, we were told that our Spanish was different and were called *manitos*. We would call each other *hermanos*, but because we used it a lot, we dropped the "her" and so *manitos*. In church, we covered the saints only during Lent (forty days) with a purple cloth. It had to do with mourning practices.

At home, during mourning, the ladies wore black mourning clothes and covered saints as well as the mirrors as a mourning custom. When someone died, people were up through the night, praying and singing, and the deceased was buried within twenty-four hours. At the funeral, people made the motion of the sign of the cross with the dirt and threw it into the grave over the casket that had been lowered already.

People stayed and visited until the next day. It was customary for neighbors and family to go back to the family home of the deceased, not more than a month later, to give them *el pésame* (condolences). We had a one-year anniversary mass and lit candles in the church. Women mourned a whole year.

On the grave itself people piled rocks, before headstones were placed. Rocks are placed over the dirt on the gravesite for the purpose of identifying the site. This was until we were able to place permanent markers.

We never read the Bible. Homes didn't have Bibles, and mass was in Latin. In my family, when a boy turned fifteen (coming of age), at a dance they would select this young boy, pick him up on their shoulders, parade him around the hall, and tell him the next dance would be in his honor because he had come of age. Now, it's done just for girls and called *Quincenaria* (*Quinceañera*).

The only time we would ask for benediction was before we went to bed. When someone went on a long journey, Dad or Mom would say, "May God be with you." *El Sábado de Gloria*, Saturday before Easter, would be the day they blessed water at the church and had it in tubs. People would come and take holy water in small decanters home and keep it through the whole year.

Cousins married cousins, even to this day. I think we are all related anyway. My husband, Willie, and I are distant cousins on the same Torres line. I went to a wedding a month ago where they were fourth cousins. We cleaned the house Friday night for Saturday and Sunday. Sunday was for churchgoing. Saturday and Sunday were considered days of rest. We dressed special for Sunday.

During rain and thunder, Mom would get holy water and sprinkle at the doors and windows. It was a blessing. She made an acclamation to Santa Barbara, protector of lightning and thunder.

Men didn't shave during Holy Week. There were no dances, no radio, or music. We baked meat, *empanaditas*, at Christmas and would wait to drink milk or water, eaten hot or when they were fresh. *Buñuelos* were eaten during Christmas. Everyone got a toy top for Christmas in my generation. On Christmas morning, we went to the neighbors and family where we were given peanuts and Christmas candy.

During Lent, we beat egg whites and put the yolk back into the white. Eggs with blood spots were thrown away. This was *torta de huevo* which was placed in the red chili sauce. We ate *sopapillas*. This was made with fresh dough. We ate *quelites* during Lent. The *quelites* were dried the spring before Lent  because they come out in spring and summer. *Verdolagas*, another dried plant like *quelites*, was eaten during Lent. Lent begins in February.

We would fast before mass on Sunday and confession on Saturday evening. No meat was served during Lent. When shoes were removed at night, they were not placed at the head of the bed because we might have bad dreams. We said grace after meals, giving thanks to God for a good meal. It was called *Gracias a Dios*.

A Jewish Star, six pointed necklace, was worn by Felicitas

Olguín, my grandmother, in a photograph with Ramón, my Grandpa Torres. This photo was taken about 1905, much after the Inquisition. These people were already associated with the pioneer Jews in Santa Fe. Jews were helping the Catholics build churches. Regarding the Jewish Star, it might have been copied from the pioneer Jews or they might have known of their heritage.

Although I have done extensive research, I am interested in researching more.

**Felipe Ortega**

The most essential belief of the Penitentes was to perform

acts of charity (*caridad*), aiding New Mexican communities. Their practice of helping those in need continues. Was this a connection to Judaism?

There was definitely a Jewish connection regarding *mitzvot*. One of the biggest concerns of the Penitentes was proper burial for the dead. This was an overriding concern of the Penitentes.

The *morada* is where the Penitentes reside, primarily during Holy Week. The *oratorio* is where they pray, usually, but not always.

My belief is that the Penitentes began because of the inability of crypto-Jews to practice Judaism openly. This was a means of achieving an end, to continue their understanding of Judaism.

It is clear to me that there is a definite connection to Judaism as indicated by the following practices: During Holy Week, the people in the community were served spinach with boiled eggs. This represented the bitter herbs served during the Passover *Seder* and were only served during Holy Week, which coincides with Passover. Also served during this week, was a cracker pudding for the unleavened bread or *matzah*. *Capirotada* is the Ladino word for *haroset*. In places other than La Madera, this dish was made with leavened bread. During Holy Week, after Holy Tuesday (Wednesday to Saturday at noon), you had to have all work done. Wood had to be chopped, and water was brought inside. You couldn't play outside or wash your hair. They had to make enough food for those three days and couldn't cook. Food could be warmed up. I think this was of the same sensibility as the *Sabbath*. They transferred the *Sabbath* prescription of no work to Holy Week. They were so far removed from Judaism that they didn't know how to follow Jewish rituals.

During Christmas, bonfires were lit for nine consecutive nights by families in La Madera, New Mexico. They were lit

# Crypto-Jews 97

from December 16 until Christmas Eve. The significance of the nine nights (candles are usually lit for eight days during *Hanukkah*) was that the *menorah* had eight candles plus the *shammash*, the servant candle used to light the other candles. This practice was created to avoid suspicion by the Inquisition and was not just practiced by the Penitentes. For this celebration, Mom remembers playing with the dreidel when she was young.

Every Catholic service, in this area, ends with a prayer for the dead. This practice does not exist anywhere else in Catholicism. A Catholic prayer was used to pray for the dead so that the people would not be suspect. For the same reason, baptismals were conducted in the Catholic Church.

My ancestors came from Spain and traveled from Mexico City to Durango, and finally to New Mexico. They brought their culture with them, and it bears little or no resemblance to Mexican culture. We don't consider ourselves Mexican. I never knew I was Jewish until a visit to Detroit where I was introduced to Judaism. I'm Jewish! I'm living in the year 2001 knowing I'm Jewish. Mom is Jewish.

There are four things which stand out in my mind that gave me clues that my family was Jewish:

1. Grandmother lit candles on Friday evening at sunset. I thought that's what Catholics do, but no Catholic families do this. I asked Grandmother about this practice, and she yelled, "Death of Christ." These words were said to let me know that I shouldn't ask everyone about this.

2. *Hanukkah*—I saw eight candles lit, one at a time, in Detroit. Why nine here? Eight would look Jewish. A similar ritual was the nine-day prayer or novena to the Baby Jesús in the Catholic Church. As for the bonfires, during the nine days of lighting them, Jewish families would dress up and gather at the schoolhouse and wear pointed hoods, exactly as inquisitors wore during the Inquisition. They would run through

the village as *abuelos,* meaning grandfather, to make sure the children knew their Catholic prayers, again to avoid suspicion from the Inquisition. We still have bonfires. We still have dreidels or *trompos* (spinning tops), used only during *Hanukkah.*

3. Grandmother lost a son and sat *shivah.* When her son died, she covered the mirrors with a black cloth, as well as covering all windows. She sat on a stool for eight days, during which time people visited. I feel this was a crypto-Jewish community where so many rituals were practiced. In Detroit, I saw what was done when my girlfriend's father died. Oh, my God, I'm Jewish! We would mourn for eight days and have a thirty-day ceremony, called *Las Honras.* My uncle did have a Catholic burial in Utah. Candles were lit in the church on the one-year anniversary of a loved-ones death. This is not done in the regular Catholic Church. Burial is done within twenty-four hours, followed by sitting *shivah.* My grandmother always dressed in black (Catholic tradition) after her husband died. These rituals were transferred over to the pueblo and are still highly regarded.

4. Holy Week (Before Easter)—The meals are all Lenten dishes (no meat). There is a presence of a cracker pudding for the unleavened bread. Elsewhere, this was made with leavened bread. *Capirotada, haroset* in Ladino, was a symbolic food during Passover.

There was another meal served outside of Holy Week, a kosher Holy Week, where wine was served, without having to be suspect for drinking wine. It was called *Brindis,* which means *mazel tov.* This practice does not continue in La Madera, but it is still done in a nearby village. The most widely sung hymn during Holy Week was the *Song of Songs,* and everyone was required to know it by heart. Why are they insistent on singing this hymn? It's one of the *mitzvot* for Passover to read the book of *The Song of Songs.* The *Haggadah* reading is part of the *mitzvot* of Passover.

More Sephardic practices continue here because this is a very conservative area. More crypto-Jews than *conversos* probably settled it. The people of Spain do not understand our language because we are speaking an ancient form of Spanish called Ladino. When the Penitentes were worshiping, the men wore black scarves on their heads, *tallit* or prayer shawls. There was a definite need to preserve Judaism, but there was never a discussion about any connection to Judaism.

**Filiberto Pacheco**

I have done extensive research into the family history, with the hope of informing descendants of Pachecos in New Mexico of their origin and the family that preceded them.  On Dad's side, Gerónimo Pacheco was the first Pacheco in New Mexico followed by twelve generations of Pachecos since his arrival in the 1600s.  He was either from Spain or Portugal.  The name Pacheco goes back to 93 B.C. when Vivio Pacheco was a general under Julius Caesar.  He came to Spain and Portugal with the conquering Roman armies.  Research revealed that Vivio probably first settled in Portugal and then in Spain, as the Pacheco families in both countries are related.

Many Pachecos in New Spain were called *conversos*.

Gerónimo was accused of practicing pagan rites in New Mexico. The only things he could have brought were Jewish rites. He came with his wife. It was reported in 1628 that he was taking part in pagan games at the San Juan Pueblo. He denied the charges.

My great-grandfather was Librado Pacheco. Grandmother was Modesta Pacheco and Grandfather was Eliseo Pacheco. I have a prayer book, written in Spanish, by Librado and Eliseo. It was rumored in the family that we're Jewish. However, it was never brought out. They were very secretive and deep into Penitente rites. They were always praying in the home in Mora, the northernmost outpost of the Spanish colonies. I went to the ranch all the time, and it's still called Pacheco. Marriages occurred within the family. First cousins married first cousins.

Grandfather prayed in Spanish. We were told that our Spanish was Ladino. We were very learned people. Education was very important. Biblical names in the family were Moisés and Eliseo.

We prepared Friday and rested on Saturday. There was a Catholic Church built on the Pacheco ranch. We never saw icons in my house. The family was always fasting and praying. Burial was within twenty-four hours. Praying was done overnight. There were seven days for mourning when visitors would bring food. The mourning period was for one year. We had a one-year anniversary mass that is still done. Candles are lit in the house. My sister does it. Our children will do this. We placed stones on headstones located at the old church on the ranch.

We didn't know of the *menorah*. When I grew up we ate *buñuelos*. They are now known as *sopapillas*. They are eaten on Christmas and special occasions. We had holy water on the doorpost that we touched when we went out.

Mom is Indian. She practiced what Dad practiced. When

slaughtering a pig, we would hang it with its head down so that the blood would drain. The throat was cut with a knife. Most animals were killed in this manner. We ate the blood.

The women stayed in the house after birth, but this is not done now.

Corn *tortillas* were eaten during Lent and Holy Week. I didn't pay any attention as to the reason for this custom. On Christmas Eve, unleavened bread was given to each member of the family at home. It was like a communion wafer. The family told us it was unleavened. This is still done. *Empanaditas* are eaten before Christmas.

Whenever we went on a trip, we kneeled before our father or grandfather, and they would bless you with the "laying of hands." This is not done in the Catholic Church. The family had old Bibles and read the Old Testament. They were superstitious. I'm the first in the family to start tracing our ancestry. To me, it's great to know. I'm a practicing Catholic and probably wouldn't change my faith. However, I would like to understand it better.

There are some Indians with the name Pacheco. Petrona Pacheco was the daughter of Felipe Pacheco. It was thought that Petrona was killed during the Indian Revolt. When the Spaniards came back, she had six children, three by an Indian and three by her husband. Taking their mother's name, they were all Pacheco.

Cousins in Mora first mentioned Jewishness. They got it from their dad, Moisés, who was ninety-six years old when he died. He died about ten years ago. They seemed to know that we're Jewish. I approached them asking if we were Jewish after researching. They said, "Well, we're Jewish." They're much older. My brother has a key that looks medieval. However, we don't know its origin.

**Flora Campos**

The names on Mom's side were Romo, García, and Gonzáles. Grandfather's parents died and he was adopted by a family named Vigil. Dad's real grandmother was Sena. Mom's side had Spanish blood, meaning from Spain. Father said he had Italian blood from his real family. On Mom's side, Great-Grandfather was Cristóbal Romo. This was unusual because of the spelling.

Dad was Catholic. Dad's real dad was blond and blue-eyed. Dad was supposed to be a Catholic but never went to church. He said he didn't have to go to church to believe in God and follow Him.

Mother's side was fair. All have light eyes, green eyes and blue eyes. All of my cousins are much older, and I can't ask them anything.

We worshiped on Sunday. Mom said that Saturday was supposed to be the *Sabbath*.

Mom said that when she was about sixteen, she became

a Protestant and was very involved in the Presbyterian Church. However, her family was Catholic with the exception of her. It was "hush-hush" that she got away from the Catholic Church. She didn't want to talk about it.

We were told that our Spanish was different. Southern New Mexicans laugh at Northern New Mexicans. In Mexico, they told me my Spanish was very different than theirs. They said that it was real Spanish, like in Spain.

We lived in Truchas and have no relatives there. There are relatives in Las Vegas, New Mexico. We do not have icons in the house. We didn't do this, but all my relatives would bless their children by placing their hands on their heads and making the sign of the cross on the forehead. This was done when anyone would leave a house.

We always said grace after meals in English and Spanish. "God is good, God is great, and we thank Him for this food. By His hand we must be fed. Give us Lord our daily bread. Amen." Wherever I went, grace was said before the meals.

*Buñuelos* were eaten during Christmas, more so at Christmas and Easter. During Lent, we ate *buñuelos* and *panocha*s (doesn't rise and is like a wheat pudding). We ate *tortas* (made with eggs and placed into red chili). We ate *quelites* and boiled eggs with *chile caribe* (a bread pudding with raisins in it). We ate *capirotada* (made with toasted bread crumbs and made into a pudding that doesn't rise).

We never had circumcision and ate pork. As soon as we cut the head of animals, we drained the blood into a pot placed by Mom. Dad ate blood. I don't eat blood and throw it away.

Father didn't allow us to hang out with kids. Mama would put chicken on wood and chop the head off. When someone died, we would keep the body in the house and not take it to church. People stayed with the body overnight. After two or three days, we would have the funeral. People would come on the day of the funeral. There was a one-year mourning period when there wouldn't be any music or dancing. I placed stones on Mama's headstone without thinking. We would sweep away from the door. Mother would not bathe for forty days after a baby was born. We weren't allowed to bathe during menstruation. In the family, we saw the bride and groom's hands bound with a white cord and a prayer was said. This was the *laco* ritual.

At home, growing up, there were big *biscochitos*. They were sugar cookies. We ate *empanaditas* all the time including Christmas and Easter. On Sundays, growing up, after church, we had company, family, where big meals were served. Mom and Dad said the minute they got there, we were not allowed to socialize with the adults at all.

When Catholic relatives visited, kids who left to go into town had the sign of the cross made on their foreheads. Mom did not do this because we were Presbyterian. We ate red chili with beef rather than with pork. In southern New Mexico, they always ate red chili with pork. We ate pork occasionally because they raised eleven kids and had to survive. Mom used beef for everything.

I would be happy to know our roots, but nothing is confirmed because we don't have any relatives to ask.

## Frank N. Larribas

On my father's side, I traced my heritage back to Father's grandfather, buried in the National Cemetery in Santa Fe. I went to the archives in Santa Fe, searching for his name and found a pay roster in the archives. It states that at the time he was eighteen years old, and it describes him as being five foot and two inches tall. He had black hair and dark eyes. The interesting thing is that when I'd look at his grave, the name is spelled with a V instead of a B. The name of my great-grandfather, Nabor Larribas or Nabor Larrivas, was not a common name.

Dad had several stories:

He used to tell me that the family originated from Louisiana. In my own thinking, it made sense because Basques moved into that area. Basques lived between France and Spain. He also said, at a later date, that we were Basque. Researching the name Larribas, I found they settled in this country very early, in the 1500s or 1600s. I read an article by someone from the Spanish Heritage Museum in Albuquerque. His research said that there were originally three brothers from

Spain. Two went to North America and one to South America. I heard from another source that the Larribas name is better known in South America than here. I did find out that there was a Captain Larribas that brought troops up from Mexico to retake Santa Fe from the Indians after the Indian revolt.

I found out from the museum source that the root name was Ribas. Ribas is a name found in Spain. La Ribas came from Leon (Lion). I found out from a book from the Mexico Heritage Museum there is a village called La Ribas. The family home is still there, and the coat of arms is in the house.

My father's grandfather was named Nabor Larribas. My grandfather was Francisco Larribas. My father's name was Nabor Larribas like his grandfather. My name is Francisco Larribas like my grandfather. The interesting thing is that when my son was born, my wife wanted to give him my first name, Frank. He is Frank Jason Larribas. But when I didn't name my son after my dad, Nabor Larribas, he was quite angry because I was breaking a tradition. Dad never spoke about his heritage. He was proud of being Spanish and Basque. He always told me to marry my own kind, meaning of the same heritage. The whole family lived on the same block (extended family).

On Mom's side, Mom is Millie Vigil, her maiden name. My grandfather was Vigil. Her father and mother married in Costia (New Mexico or Colorado). They eventually lived in Colorado. She told me stories that her grandmother would tell her— stories of coming west in a covered wagon.

Mother's father, Tomasio Vigil, said only that his father had five sheep ranches in Colorado. He wasn't educated but was self-taught. He was very wealthy. He was president of the bank in Walsenberg, Colorado. He bought the first car in Walsenberg. The thinking in my family was that you tell kids nothing. When adults spoke, the kids were outside. My father wasn't religious. My grandmother had an altar and she would pray and light candles every night. As a child, she listened to the rosary and read the Bible. My family said to "Keep the *Sabbath* Holy." This was Sunday. There was no work, nothing on Sunday. Father felt once I made my Holy Communion, he didn't care what happened.

My father's grandparents were Catholic and went to church. My father was Catholic and never did. Mother was not Catholic. There was a conflict however. He did not allow her to go to her church, but he wanted her to be a Catholic. Yet he never went. My brother, Hubert, is a half-brother. He wasn't raised with the family. When Dad and his first wife were divorced, she took Hubert to Arizona. My mom is his third wife. I didn't meet Hubert until I was ten. Dad said never to drink milk in the summertime. The reason was that it would curdle in my stomach because of the heat. Parents had stories to frighten children when we got together with the family. They said Yorona, a Gypsy lost a baby who drowned. At night she looked for it and would steal children. Gypsies would steal children. They're none around here.

Grandmother on Grandmother's side, my great-grandmother would tell a story about a man who would go around with a burlap sack. He would take bad kids in the sack, and they'd never be seen again.

Mother lived on a sheep ranch. I learned to kill animals from my father. We would hang the sheep from the hind legs, slit their throats, and allow the blood to drain. We twirled the chicken until it was decapitated. Eggs with blood spots were thrown out. Mother and Grandmother would sweep inward.

When I was young, when a person died, we displayed the body at home. Mourners would go to the house to pray the rosary. The deceased was buried on the third day. There was a rosary for two nights. People came to the house for a couple of days after the burial and brought food.

We ate *panochas* during Lent. We ate *buñuelos* at

Christmas and all the time. During Holy Week, the week before Easter, Good Friday, we didn't do much.

Grandfather had a Bible full of pictures. Years later, I found out his story was untrue. He showed pictures portraying Moses and the Jews crossing the Red Sea. Two or three pictures away, the Egyptians and chariots were chasing them. He interpreted the pictures, indicating that these were Catholics running away from the Egyptians. Somewhere in his lifetime someone told him this story. This story was only in Grandfather's house on Dad's side. I found out the true story of Moses and the Jews running and crossing the Red Sea. I was eight or nine. I was very close to my grandfather.

My understanding of Catholicism was that it was a secretive religion. They didn't tell you everything. All the preaching was done in Latin. I had no idea what was going on. I left the Catholic Church and went to the Presbyterian Church. What kept me going back to the Presbyterian Church were the stories of the Old Testament (David and Goliath). I was about eight or nine years old. The family didn't like it. I've always thought I don't know if I have this Jewish heritage.

As a child my first language was Spanish. Albuquerque public school policy was to teach English. Spanish was unacceptable. I can remember having teachers with Spanish surnames who would totally ignore my speaking to them in Spanish. There were times I would walk out and go home because I could not express that I needed to go to the bathroom. I have been told my Spanish was incorrect because I didn't speak as they did. I was called *mochos*, clipped. I spoke a clipped Spanish. I was taught old Spanish from Grandfather, Father's father, who originated in Rowe, New Mexico. I was told by people from southern New Mexico about old Spanish.

My grandfather retired from the railroad. He used to go to Mexico to party in the summer. It was accepted. He didn't consider himself a Mexican. All my family takes offense to being called Mexican. I don't know when they came to New Mexico. The biggest problem is that Larribas is not a common name.

## Frutoza López

Mom said we came from Spain. Mother was Córdova and Rodríguez. Her first name was Rebecca. Dad was Romero and Archuleta. Dad was a sheepherder and was gone a lot. I grew up in Truchas with the extended family. We were sent to boarding school. Education was very important to Dad. Mom lit candles on Easter. The *Sabbath* was Sunday, and she would clean the house on Saturday night, getting ready for Sunday. We would fast every other Saturday night. We believed in circumcision. Dad died in the hospital and was brought home for one night. We put a nickel or quarter to close the eyes of the deceased. Burial was the next day. People threw handfuls of dirt into the grave. They still do it.

We had a one-year mourning period and lit candles on the one-year anniversary of a person's death. We didn't have music all year. We swept towards the center of the house.

Pigs, cows, and chickens were shot when killed. These animals were then hung to drain the blood into the ground. We covered the blood with the earth. Father ate the blood. The rest of us didn't. I thought it was gross. We ate pork. If eggs had a blood spot, we removed the spot and ate the egg. We salted pork. After birth, the women in the family stayed in the house forty days. There was no bathing allowed. My parents would bless the children as they kneeled. They placed one hand on the child's head and made the sign of the cross in front of him. We played with a top that had a string all the time, but mostly in the summer. We ate *panocha* during Lent. *Buñuelos* were eaten all the time. We were active in the Catholic Church, and Dad belonged to the Penitentes.

When we were young, you weren't supposed to have a Bible. The mass was in Latin. I didn't know what was going on. I didn't understand Latin. Mother would recite her rosary with everyone. Dad prayed silently by himself in a corner of the house for an hour. He didn't read anything. Mom went to mass every Sunday. Dad went a few times out of respect for Mom. When he didn't go, he sat by himself praying very quietly. The female relatives covered their heads with shawls or hats in church.

I don't know if I have this heritage.

**Geneva Márquez Rael**

Names in the family are Padilla, Vallejos, Baca, and Martínez. My father never would mention his family. Grandfather used to make us sit down in the living room and tell us stories about the old days. He'd tell us, "One of these days we'll all be gone and you won't know anything about your ancestors." Mom's dad, Prajedes Martínez, was a storyteller.

One story was that we came from Jews. He'd tell us about my dad's father, Liberato Márquez. Dad's family was odd. They would never mention their family from the past. We didn't know if they had brothers or sisters. They were very secretive, and we knew nothing from them. Mom's dad told us how Dad's family (Liberato's family) would cover their windows in black around Christmas. Liberato prayed in the dark rooms. Grandpa Martínez, Mom's dad, was a Penitente. Penitentes pray on Friday night and during Holy Week. The men would lock themselves up in the *morada* during Holy Week, and all they did was pray. This was before Easter. Women would bring coffee to them. They ate bland food and fasted.

Mom's dad said we were descendants from Spanish Jews. There's a part of Spain where people have light coloring and a part where people have dark coloring. We're light people. Grandfather was tall and had red hair and blue eyes. Grandfather Martínez and Mom's family spoke of Grandfather Liberato as if he was special. He was very secretive.

Both families came straight to New Mexico—to Saboyeta, Moquino, Piedra, Lumbre, and Márquez. They never went through Mexico. We were told that Grandfather Márquez, my grandfather, came from Spain, and the Spanish took him on a raid to an Indian village. He saw an Indian girl and fell in love. He married her, and she was our grandmother. Dad was a churchgoer. I was told by Mom that Dad's father (Márquez) would get up in the middle of the night and pray in a dark room. Mom wasn't allowed in there. Dad prayed in the bedroom. He was very private, and we weren't allowed in.

We ate *buñuelos* mostly in the winter. We believed in circumcision. Mom's family tried to make a son a priest. The deceased stayed in the house for two nights, and we prayed the rosary. We had the burial on the third day. The immediate family would sit in the house for a week. People visited and brought food. There was one year of mourning. We would say mass on the year anniversary of a person's death. The immediate family throws handfuls of dirt in the grave during the burial. The older people still do it. The younger people don't do this.

I had a traumatic situation in junior high. The teacher asked for my last name. I answered that it was Márquez. She yelled, "It's not Márquez. It's Marcus. I'm sick and tired of people like you hiding that you're Jewish." The teacher was an Anglo. Dad was a janitor at the high school next door.

He had me taken back to the classroom. He went in, but I couldn't hear what was said. He stayed in the class for a long time, but he wouldn't explain anything to me.

We lived on a farm. When killing animals, we hung them by their hind legs and killed them with a sharp knife. We used special knives for this and drained the blood. We also cooked the blood. Eggs with blood spots were thrown out. We salted meat when we were ready to cook. My dad raised animals, but he wasn't a meat eater.

During Lent, we ate *panocha* and blue corn *tortillas*. The corn *tortillas* are made with corn and water. They were eaten for Ash Wednesday and Good Friday. We ate *quelites* during Lent. It was wild spinach. No meat was allowed. We also ate flour *tortillas*. Mirrors were covered Ash Wednesday and Good Friday. The Church and the Penitentes cover the crucifix and saints with a black cloth during Holy Week, before Easter.

After birth, the women stayed in the house for six weeks and didn't bathe. My parents' generation did this.

Grandfather (Mom's side) would put his hand on our heads and make a cross. We knelt. At home, especially if you were sick, you were sprinkled with holy water from the church.

The Catholic Church did not allow us to have Bibles. Dad told us Bible stories. He told us about Moses. Father was so happy with the Ten Commandments movie. He took us to see the movie and told us what he remembered from growing up.

Growing up, we were told that my grandfather's ancestors came from Spain, running away from the Spanish, something about Jews. They weren't clear on it. People around here told us our Spanish was different. Dad and Mom had us learn English when we were young. I've always questioned my Jewish heritage. I believe I have it. It wouldn't change me in any way.

## Gerald González

The emergence of my consciousness of having a Jewish heritage was a gradual occurrence. I was given a traditional parochial school upbringing as a child. I noticed, however, that my father did not seem to relate well, though he was also raised in a "traditional" Catholic family, to church-connected matters. He did not attend mass very often, and he ate meat on Fridays. I also learned as I grew up that his great-grandfather, my great-great-grandfather, whose name was Tomás Gonzáles, had studied for the priesthood in his youth. He never completed his studies and married instead.

While he served in the Army Air Corps during World War II, one of my father's best friends was someone from New York whose name, if I recall correctly, was Abe Goldberg. I also noticed, as I grew older, that the pattern of not being deeply involved, personally, in church-related matters was repeated by my grandfather's behavior, my father's father.

I spent many years researching my own family history. During the course of my research, I gradually became aware that the Inquisition had been active in Mexico as well as parts of the Southwest, like New Mexico where I grew up. Then I attended a lecture  given by a Professor Liebman and a Hispanic professor at St. Mary's College in San Antonio, Texas, where I was stationed with the U.S. Air Force.  Professor Liebman described the sixteenth and seventeenth century crypto-Jewish community in Mexico City, and the other professor spoke about crypto-Jewish indicators in the Spanish-speaking community around Monterrey, Mexico. The latter described customs such as marking a visit to a loved-one's grave by leaving a small stone as a marker on the headstone, or not mixing certain foods together at meals, or turning mirrors to the wall when someone in a household dies. And I realized that, while I was not familiar with many of the customs being described, these three were familiar to me.

At that point, it began to dawn on me that there was at least some possibility that I had some Jewish blood in my family.  I continued my research (in 1972 or 1973) with a growing suspicion that this was true. I exchanged information with others doing similar work.  I discovered, in the process, that my family surname came from Portugal at a time that Portuguese settlers in the New World were viewed with suspicion because of the possibility that they were not only conversos, but also practicing crypto-Jews. I discovered that two of my ancestors had been imprisoned in the early 1660s by the Inquisition for possibly engaging in heretical practices. And I noticed that in the seventeenth century history of New Mexico, the members of my Gonzáles family line consistently allied themselves with the secular, rather than the clerical side of New Mexico's Spanish colonial government.

Several years ago, as I was explaining my research and my suspicions to some first cousins, my youngest paternal aunt, who had been listening intently, broke in and said something like, "Yes, our family came here because they were being persecuted for being practicing Jews!" I later explored how she came to know this, and she reminded me that, as the youngest daughter, she had spent many hours listening to my grandfather talk about the family just before he died. During some of these conversations, he told her about our family's Jewish heritage. It probably explains the remark my grandfather once made to me when I had just begun to research our family history more intensely, "If I were not a Catholic, I would be a Jew."

The dawning of my awareness of my Jewish family history, my connection as a Sephardim, emerged in such a way that I did not have to confront it with the same kind of surprise that I am aware many others have had to deal with. Consequently, I have been able to embrace it as part of my identity.

**Gloria Córdova**

My paternal grandfather, José Benito Córdova, was born in 1884. Dad, Louis Barrón Córdova, was the oldest of his children that survived (three out of five survived). Héctor, the youngest of three who survived, moved to California. He would come home and have to leave. It was an emotional departure for the family with lots of drama for fear that they wouldn't see him again. Uncle Héctor married and lived in California. On his annual visit, he knelt for Grandpa's blessing as Grandpa would place his hands over the heads of my uncle and his family before they would leave. Grandpa Córdova always blessed his children in that manner when they left to travel. I was not aware that this was a custom of Jewish origin.

There was exceptional secretiveness on the Barrón side, Dad's mother's family, where the second child of three that survived was raised by the Barróns after their mother died. That was Aunt Virginia, called Nina. Dad was eight years old when his mother died. He and his brother, Héctor, were raised by Grandpa's Córdova family. This family would speak behind closed doors and was very secretive, but he didn't know what they were secretive about.

Grandfather Córdova was the oldest of his brothers and sisters, Donaciano's children. Most of those children remained single and all lived together. In the house, during prayer time, they'd all gather in the parlor room off to the side. It was a room seldom used. I was three when Donaciano, my great-grandfather died. They prayed in Spanish. I was told that our Spanish was different. Our Colorado family commented that some of the relatives "spoke like New Mexicans."

Father said that Mom doesn't have Mexican blood even though her father's family was from Zacatecas, Mexico. Her paternal grandfather, Alvino Carmona, stayed in Mexico. Her father, Catarino Carmona, came to the United States. Spanish people here called themselves Mexican until they realized it would be used against them, perhaps because of color. This was Mom's family.

Dad's great-grandfather, Bonifacio Barrón, was naturalized in Taos in 1871. He emigrated from Chihuahua,

Mexico. It was never said that we came from Spain, but it was emphasized, "You're Spanish." Mom said, "Remember your mother tongue."

Mom had holy water on the doorpost. She made the sign of the cross when she went in and out. You had to bless yourself when you went in and out. The men and an aunt made fun of her.

Mom said, "Your grandfather next to God." Donaciano's parents spoke of *morada*s. Our family is reverential of *morada*s. In my generation, friends of the neighborhood gathered in homes to pray. It was not secret at that time.

The men avoided church. There were icons, statues, and pictures of saints in the home. Father said, "This place looks like a cathedral." He objected to so many holy pictures. The Catholic Church in my childhood didn't want you to read the Bible.

In the old times, if someone died, the body was kept in the home for a few days. People threw handfuls of dirt into the grave on top of the coffin. I remember hearing that mirrors were covered by paternal great-grandparents. The grandparents would sit in the house for a few days. Dad's sister's youngest daughter died in 1999. It was not part of the culture to date someone else before the year was up. Her family was incensed because the year was not up, and her husband was seeing another woman. There was a mass on the year anniversary of a person's death based upon the decision of the family. A candle would be lit on the altar in the home.

Dad says, "*Todos son primos y primas.*" We're all connected; we're all related. Cousins married cousins. The old generation got married, especially people from Taos (*Taoseños*), under the *huppah*. That was my great-great-grandparents' generation.

Dad was raised on a farm. In his family, the older generations (great-grandparents and beyond) salted meat. If you spoke badly of someone you were referred to as a *Marrano*. In the older generations, the women couldn't get up for a long time after childbirth. Everything passed on to the family was through the women.

Education was stressed, one of the reasons I'm earning my doctorate at this stage of my life. Great-Grandmother's family, Donaciano's mother was Marina Rivera. Her sister, Damiana, married a prominent man (Casimiro Barela), senator in Colorado for forty years. He was sent from his home as a very young boy to live with a priest in another village who educated him.

Mother's maternal grandmother was Petra. Mom would tell the story that her Grandmother Petra's grandfather carried keys, and he was the village teacher. The village teacher was highly esteemed. The keys were very important to him. Petra told Cora the story.

There was a system called *Compadrazco*. That's a system where the sponsors or godparents for children's baptism are carefully chosen to keep the land within the family. They were like executors of a will.

Chickens were killed by twirling and decapitation. Dad would collect *quelites*.

Mother went to confession on Friday, late afternoon. She wasn't ready for Sunday unless she went to confession. The *Sabbath* was Sunday. Mom said that Grandmother threw salt during storms. My mother wished to be connected to the roots of the Bible.

I believe I have the connection to Judaism. As for conversion, I'm not inclined. I feel connected to part of the heritage. Why am I so interested? Genealogically, my interest is in being connected through the mothers. It's in my spirit.

These mothers all speak through me. I saw them like a dream with scarves over their heads when I received my doctorate.

**Joe Austin**

Grandfather Edward Austin raised me. His side has people from Ireland. Grandmother, on Mother's side, believed that her parents were from Spain. Her maiden name was Aragón. Her mother's maiden name was Martínez.

My grandparents were secretive. You never asked questions, and they never told you anything. If they wanted you to know something, they'd tell you. If elders spoke, children had to go elsewhere. We always prayed together at home in the mornings and evenings. We belonged to the Catholic Church.

I was raised in Arizona, and the Spanish from Mexico was different. I'd spend time in New Mexico, and friends in New Mexico said I spoke differently.

I heard that part of the family came through Texas two hundred years ago. We ate *buñuelos* any time. We hung larger animals to drain the blood. We also cooked the blood. Eggs with blood spots were given to animals. We killed chickens by twirling them until they were decapitated. We didn't believe in circumcision.

We buried the dead the next day. Women lined the coffin. We had a rosary that night. People visited before and after the burial and brought food. We prayed and lit candles on the year anniversary of a person's death and on their birthday. We bought these candles in a store and lit them in the house. When I was a child, I remember covering the mirrors when someone died. It's in the back of my mind. Family members probably did it. Everyone was related to someone. We made our own headstones. My wife's grandfather carved lambs and doves on the headstones.

My nephew, Aaron, has a Biblical name.

During Lent, Holy Week, there was no activity. Kids weren't supposed to speak, and music was not permitted. We ate *torta de huevo,* eggs fried in a skillet with chili added. No meat was eaten at this time. My grandparents said if you were making a racket you were causing our Lord pain. We wouldn't chop wood or anything that would make noise during Holy Week.

I've been in Bernalillo, New Mexico, since 1973 and was born in Santa Rosa, New Mexico. I was brought up to believe God comes first, before everything. Only God knows if I have any Jewish heritage.

### Joe Cisneros

I believe that my father was either Spanish or Portuguese. My father's mother told me that they were Portuguese and Indian. My mother's side was González. Cisneros is Portuguese or Spanish.

My family did not avoid church or icons. If someone died, there was a one-year mourning period. They prayed every day and were not permitted to have music and dances. My grandmother, aunt, and the old ladies wore shawls. The ladies covered their heads in church. You didn't see this in regular Catholicism.

Animals were slaughtered with special knives and then hung upside down to drain the blood. I do it. If a blood spot was seen in an egg, the egg was thrown out. Any food that fell to the floor was not eaten.

I believe in God and Church. There is probably a connection to Judaism. On Friday night, we cooked and cleaned the house. We couldn't work on Saturday or Sunday. We didn't eat meat on Friday.

My mother and father told me to "Keep the *Sabbath* (Saturday) holy." I was brought up to go to church. My mother would say, "The Lord our God, The Lord is one."

The family made unleavened bread for Lent. Mexican Spaniards ate blood sausage. My family did not eat it and avoided blood. They did not eat catfish because of the whiskers and because they are scavengers. They did not eat any animals with claws. Maybe that's all I remember.

## John García

There are seven brothers in my family. My oldest brother,

Ralph, and I reverted to Judaism about two-and-a-half years ago. My brother, David García, a Superior Court Judge in California, born between us, reverted to the religion of our ancestors about twenty years ago when he married Louise Rosen, an Ashkenazi Jew. He has two children and the whole family follows the Jewish religion.

Reversion means to return. Many people with our ancestry are offended by the need to convert. *Anusim* resent having to go through conversion because they, or rather their ancestors, were forced to convert. As a consequence, many are not returning to Judaism. We (Ralph and I) believe that since we are not members of an ethnic grouping or of a religion, going through a conversion process is very necessary. We were raised Roman Catholics, and therefore were in need of an education in the faith of our ancestors in order to properly revert to it.

Ralph and I resisted the Messianics. We were deeply entrenched in Catholicism and felt that Messianism was just another form of Christianity.

I've known about our Jewish heritage since I was very young, although it was never openly discussed. Our mother is a devout Catholic. Initially, our reversion caused her distress and unhappiness. She knew all along that Ralph had left Catholicism many years before, but I suppose she had hopes that he would get back later in life. Mom is now openly accepting of our reversion and has accompanied us several times to temple.

Mother's name is María Elena Acosta Perea. Both grandparents were Perea (spelled Pereyra on some of the older Mexican certificates). Our father is García Perea. Our father openly identified with Jews and the Israeli cause. Ralph's study of our genealogy and the fact that so many of our Jewish ancestors married within the family, proves to him that our parents (and my mother's brother Héctor) were unconsciously following our heritage concerning intermarriage.

Our maternal aunt and my father made us aware of our Jewish heritage. We never tried to approach the Jewish community because we never thought it was within our reach. Our maternal grandmother, María Perea, was very proud of the fact that the Jewish ladies of her generation in El Paso would often think of her as a Jew, but since I can remember, we thought of Jews as a very exclusive group. Ralph and I made a move toward Judaism subsequent to Ralph's discovery of our Jewish roots, after discussing this fact with Jewish friends, and finally, after a friend told us about getting in touch with Rabbi Bach. I gave Ralph the phone number, and after a little trepidation, he made the phone call. We've never looked back.

We are descendants of Lucas García, on my paternal side, Diego Pérez de Acosta, on my maternal side, and Juan de Perea, both of our grandmothers' ancestor. Diego Pérez de Acosta was a Portuguese Jew who ended up in Parral, Chihuahua, Mexico in 1630 during the discovery of silver. Juan de Perea was a Spanish Jew who was in on the conquest of Nueva Galicia (the Guadalajara, Mexico area) in 1525.

Lucas García was a member of the oldest Jewish settlement in the New World. A relative of his was Luis de Carvajal who was the governor of El Nuevo Reino de León, a vast area of northeastern Mexico that was granted to him by the King of Spain. This Jewish settlement was at present-day Monterrey, Nuevo León, Mexico. Among the settlers were Baltazar Castaño de Sosa, his wife Inéz Rodríguez, and his young family. These were the parents of Lucas García. When the Inquisition arrested Luis Carvajal in about 1592, the settlers scattered, some of them changing their names. Lucas Rodríguez Castaño de Sosa became Lucas García; Baltazar, his father, became Baltazar de Sosa; his mother dropped her complete surname and became Inéz Rodríguez (instead of Inéz Rodríguez de Carvajal). Inéz Rodríguez was related to the mother of a nephew of Carvajal and to Carvajal, the governor.

Luis de Carvajal, the governor, was tried and convicted of having associated with Jews, and prior to his sentence being carried out (he was to be exiled from Mexico for five years), he died in prison of "a broken heart," according to the chronicler. Luis de Carvajal, the nephew (referred to as "El Mozo" in the history books), acted as rabbi of the congregation for a time at San Luis.

The terror of the Inquisition was so intense, that our ancestors dropped many of their Jewish practices. Practices were prohibited, and the Jewish heritage was blurred. We came from *Marrano* families, keeping in the back of our minds that we were Jewish.

My ancestor's aunt, had her arm twisted eight times around before telling the inquisitors what they wanted to hear—that she was a professing Jew. She confessed and was burned at the stake for being "an obstinate and perfidious Jew." The incident has been recorded in Mexican Inquisition records. Our ancestors saw what happened and went undercover.

In 1590, Luis Carvajal, El Mozo, made penance to the Inquisition and said, "OK, we'll become Christians." But he never stopped his activities as a rabbi. His religion was not perfect. By the time of his generation, there were no materials to teach the faith. He didn't have much in the way of ritual. Still he persevered. Finally in about 1596, he was burned at the stake for following his religion. Prior to his being killed, he defiantly told the inquisitors that there were only a handful of Christians in Mexico and that the vast majority of the Spaniards were in fact Jews.

Lucas García, our direct ancestor, was known as *Capitán de la Paz* (Peace). The natives loved him. He learned the native languages; he believed in equality and peace with the natives; he helped negotiate peace treaties with them. Grandfather Rafael, Father's father, and my father were Masons in northern Mexico, Chihuahua. Grandfather was irreverent to Christians (especially priests and nuns) and not a practicing Catholic. The Masons were not beholding to the pope.

Growing up, our mother and her sisters were and still are very entrenched in the Catholic religion. Yet, her parents were not devout. Most of our ancestors believed in circumcision though. My grandfather, Rafael, was circumcised. My great-grandfather, Jesus Acosta, Mother's grandfather, was circumcised. My father was circumcised. I honestly do not know if they knew why they were circumcised. It was just a family tradition. In my immediate family, it was done in the hospital, but I had to inform the medical doctor to do it because we're Jewish. Otherwise, it wouldn't have been done.

My wife is Native American. She believes I have a Jewish heritage. All of my children respect and honor me. They have attended temple with me. I can't force anyone to become Jewish, but I can lead by example.

Ralph and I decided years ago and had discussions for years about being Jewish. Finally, we decided to stop talking and do something. I've always followed Rabbi Leon because of his leadership in initiating programs to educate crypto-Jews about their heritage. He has spoken in many countries and is well-known for understanding the plight of crypto-Jews.

We're Sephardic Jews. I've felt this in spirit and body. Now that I made the change, I am more spiritual. Judaism fits me more readily. While attending the Catholic Church, I heard things I didn't believe. I didn't know what Judaism was. The turning point for me was when Pope John Paul II said, "We are all children of God, and we all have equal paths to God." He apologized for what the Inquisition did to our ancestors. I felt liberated by this act of the pope to study

Judaism, and once I began to study my heritage, I embraced it.

I went to the synagogue on *Tisha B'Av*, and that cemented my decision to return. Now I was on another path. Richard Santos spoke here in El Paso during the *Tisha B'Av* ceremony. Although our reversion started before, this event convinced me that I was on the right path in becoming a Jew. Santos was another authority that came up with the same facts that were discovered through my brother's research.

I was initially insecure about wearing the Star of David, and wasn't fully cognizant of what Judaism was. Now, I wear it proudly.

My wife is very encouraging. When I made the change, she couldn't understand why I was identifying with white people. Messianics have literature appealing to the Sephardic Jews. For me to go to them was like accepting the conditions of the inquisitor. This is how I explained it to my wife. It was a struggle to let go of Jesus and reject the conditions of the inquisitor. Crypto-Jews continued to be Christian out of fear and ignorance. My spouse believes Messianics are Jews. I have a full-blooded Indian wife who says the Messianics are "your people" because they are openly appealing to descendants of Sephardim to join them. Here it is easier to make the transition from Christianity to Judaism. We see more people like us in Messianic congregations than in synagogues because they don't have to give up Jesus.

I believe the Catholic Church is so strong in Latin America because of the Inquisition. The Inquisition lives well because so many Christians won't accept your return to Judaism. A few weeks ago, on September 11, 2002, there was an interfaith service at Temple Mt. Sinai to signify the remembrance of the terrorist attack on the World Trade Center in New York City. Present at that service was the head of the Peace and Justice Commission of the diocese of El Paso. This man asked if I attend services in the synagogue. My response was that I do and that the services are beautiful. He told me that he objected to my coming to these services. There is a need to remove the stigma of accepting Judaism within the Catholic community and gain acceptance from the pope.

In our home, we stood in front of our parents as they gave us the blessing with the sign of the cross. This was usually done when we were taking a journey or departing.

Burial within our family was right away, within twenty-four hours. There was a one-year mourning period which was less practiced here than in Mexico. We lit candles in the church on the one-year anniversary of a person's death and paid for a mass. This is still done today by descendants of *conversos*. We placed stones on headstones when visiting the graves of loved ones. Mirrors were covered when someone died by our grandparents, in both Father's family and Mother's family. Once, when a relative died in Chihuahua, my mother assisted in the cleansing of the body and wrapping it in a shroud.

In the family, some ate blood and pork to show they were not Jewish. During the Lenten period, we ate eggs, *panocha*, *capirotada,* and corn *tortillas.* We lit bonfires nine nights before Christmas. We spun *trompos* (tops) around Christmas.

Education was very important. Father always said, "They could take everything you acquire in your life except what you are taught." We were taught to aspire. Father was a frustrated attorney. He always taught that his sons should be attorneys for the Mexican people of El Paso because Mexicans were mostly poor and needed representation from their own people.

We only spoke English, but Father used some Ladino words.

My ancestors came to El Paso because our people were victimized by Pancho Villa.

We were ostracized because we were lighter people. We weren't poor and had strong character. Actually, we were more European. We worked hard, and people who worked hard acquired things. Both sides of the family left Mexico because of the revolution.

We had a strong identity with the people of Mexico and consider ourselves part of the people of Mexico. Lucas García, *Capitán de La Paz*, thought himself a man of the people. Our tradition was to be with the people. Lucas García felt we were Mexican. Being less *mestizo* made us stand out in the Mexican community. The upper classes in Mexico were more white. We didn't have a lot of traditions because of Lucas. The family probably decided to hide completely. There have been at least fifteen generations since Lucas.

You asked why I returned to Judaism, and I thought about it. Many people do not feel the need to go back. It was easy for me to go back. We're lawyers and want to do what is legal. If that's the requirement, meaning returning to Judaism formally, we want to do what is legal to become Jews and erase the distinction between those who had forsaken Judaism (*Marranos*) and those who were officially part of Judaism.

I feel that I am home.

## Joseph Salazar

How did I know that I was a Sephardic Jew? When I was a child I was called "*todo Sefado*" which is a derivative of *Sefardita* (Sephardic Jew in Spanish). I always assumed that this was a derogatory saying that meant completely crazy. "You're the most *Judío* (Jewish)," my mother or dad would accuse each other whenever they argued. This vocabulary was part of my lifestyle as I was growing up. (These negative remarks could have been inherited by a group of people whose ancestors had been exposed to the Inquisition during their lifetime.)

We had a precious granddaughter who died of a rare disease called Battens. The information given to my daughter in California indicated that the people who are most afflicted by this disease are of Jewish or Scandinavian heritage. (It is interesting to note that Amsterdam, Holland, took a very active part in rescuing and harboring Spanish Jews during the Inquisition. Many Spanish Jews resided there and were able to openly practice Judaism in Holland.)

When I was a little boy, I used to play with a toy called *dron-dron* (dreidel). It was made out of a spool of thread with a point at the bottom. At the top of the spool there was a wooden handle used to spin it. This toy has always been identified as having a Jewish origin.

When I behaved mischievously as a child, the adults would tell me that *Elohenu* was going to get angry with me. *Eloheynu* was a Spanish equivalent to *Elohim* which means God in Hebrew. This was not really part of a Roman Catholic worship vocabulary. This word had to be passed down by those who referred to God as *Elohim.*

Another phrase that is found in some Spanish vocabulary is "*véte a la Porra*" used particularly when a child or adult is annoying someone. Many Hispanics define this as "get lost," and *porra* is associated with the *Diáspora* (the scattering of the Jews). I related it to seeking the *Torah's* help since the accused person was annoying or mischievous.

We worshiped on the Passover called *Pascua* in Spanish. It is interesting to note that the Spanish Bibles do not use the word Easter or its derivatives in Spanish as they do in the English Bibles, but use Passover instead. In our private prayer gatherings in homes, there was a mixture of Judaism and Catholicism. There usually was a rosary and a special prayer book called a *siddur*. There were always Hispanic people who had first names such as Moisés/Moshe, Solomón, Rubén, Jacobo, Elías, etc. If you read the history of the Inquisition, naming the children Old Testament names (Jewish *Tanakh*) was not encouraged—only the names from the *B'rit Hadashah* (New Covenant or New Testament) were to be used.

Another crypto-Jewish custom was to sweep the floor away from the door. We believe this was done to respect the *mezuzah* that was usually attached to the door or had been at one time part of the Sephardic lifestyle. Many older Hispanics still remember that after the birth of a child, we abstained from marital relations for forty days. Some of the women incorporated the custom also of not taking the child out in public until the forty days was completed for protection of its health.

We lit candles on Christmas. This might have been done because of the crypto-Jewish custom of lighting candles. Because of the persecution and the outlawing of circumcision, most of the crypto-Jewish men in the Southwest were not circumcised according to *Torah*. Although by Jewish tradition we would be considered out of the covenant, there are those of us who are still Jewish in spirit. Some of us believe that *Yeshua* is the *mashiach* and thus we worship with the Jewish traditions—celebrating all the feasts including *Shabbat*—in a Messianic Jewish Synagogue.

When somebody passed away, we had a wake called the *velorio*. It comes from the word *vela* meaning candle, but it also means vigil or watching, staying awake for a purpose. I remember my mother asking if the corpse had been wrapped. They put buttons on their eyelids. As Catholics, the *velorio* lasted three days to commemorate the death and resurrection of *Yeshua*. We also covered the mirrors during this time. Covering the mirrors was done, according to tradition, so that the mourners need not be reminded of their grief-altered appearance and are not tempted to vanity.

There was a prayer that was said equivalent to the *Shema* in Ladino Spanish:
*Ken no hay como nuestro Dios.*
*Ken no hay como nuestro Señor.*
*Ken no hay como nuestro Rey.*
*Ken no hay como nuestro Salvador.*

**Juan Estevan Arellano**

My mother revealed most of the following information to me.

The names in the family are Arellano, Archuleta, Durán, and Sánchez. I remember people saying that Grandmother Durán, on Mother's side, was Jewish. Relatives told this to me. My ancestors, on this side of the family, came in 1598. The Arellanos came from Mexico (Aguascaliente, Mexico). Relatives said that the Arellanos, my father's family, came from Spain in 1695 with Don Diego De Vargas who reclaimed New Mexico for Spain, without bloodshed. They also came with Alonso Rael De Aguilar, their ancestor. I believe they were probably all related or part of an extended family. The

Arellano branch of my family came from Arellano, near the Basque region and close to Pamplona.

When a bad storm was brewing, you were told to go outside and get salt to make a cross.

When someone died, Mother said her family would cover the mirrors or turn them to face the wall. They would have a twenty-four hour burial, and the mourning period would last for a year. During that time they were not allowed to go to dances or listen to the radio.

I avoid church and don't worship, as did my father. I don't believe in organized religion. At one time, the Arellanos were Protestant. The Arellanos never went to church and never had *santos* (statues). My mother said she became an Apostolic Fundamentalist because, in the Catholic Church, you were not allowed to read the Old Testament. Afterwards, my mother, sisters, and brothers became Seventh Day Adventists. Father never became part of this.

When the sun went down on Friday night, the Arellanos wouldn't do anything until Saturday evening. My brothers and sisters still do this.

The slaughtered animal would be hung so that the blood would drain. Special knives were used for butchering. Eggs with blood spots were thrown out. Mom didn't eat blood and avoided blood in food.

If bread (*tortilla*) fell to the floor, the family would throw it away.

I don't feel any connection to Judaism. However, I'm proud of my heritage and tell my children that they have an Apache, Basque, and Jewish heritage.

Why would you come here if you weren't escaping anything?

**Kim Delgado**

For some reason, I have always been intrigued by the crypto-Jewish research they are doing on Sephardic Jews. I have no idea why and still don't.

Kim is a nickname. My real name is Aurora Gloria Casimira Delgado. The names on my mother's side are Flores, Castellano, Apodaca, and Ulibarri. My mother was Castellano. Names on my dad's side are Sánchez, Delgado, García, Ortiz, and C de Baca (originally Cabeza de Baca).

Things were kept secret and people didn't discuss things the way they do now. You would never talk about psychological things. You wouldn't talk about personal things.

My aunt said the family was from Spain. There were a couple of brothers who wanted to seek their fortune. They were also seeking a better life in the New World. She had no proof, but this is what she was told.

I was thinking about one of my grandmas. She never went anywhere, including church. I thought, "How come if you're Catholic, you don't go to church?" She would pray her rosary and not go to church. I asked my aunt why Grandma didn't go to church if she was Catholic. She said, "Well, Grandma doesn't like to go anywhere." She stayed at home. I thought that was strange. She was C de Baca and García.

The people in my village, a village that is no longer there, would marry within the community because they never went anywhere. The name of the village was Chaperita, 35 miles southeast of Las Vegas. We married within our own.

We had a twenty-four hour burial. From the day that the person died, people would start coming over with food. A few days after the burial, people would still come and bring food. We had a one-year mourning period. Every year they would offer a Catholic mass for the deceased. If someone was killed at the side of the road, they would place a cross there and hold it up with a pile of rocks. They covered the mirrors after the death, and Grandma covered the mirrors during lightning. Coins were placed on the eyes of the deceased to close them.

After slaughtering animals, they would hang them and let them bleed. If my mom opened an egg with a blood spot, she would get rid of it.

After birth, women would not wash or go out in public. The women would cover their heads if they went to church.

During Holy Week, you couldn't shave. Holy Week starts on Monday and ends on the Friday before Easter Sunday. We would not do any chores. The Friday of Holy Week was the most important day. The Saturday before Easter you would be able to resume all activities. That Saturday is called Glorious Saturday.

I am intrigued by Judaism. If I discovered the truth, it would not change me. I would accept it and work with it because it identifies you.

**Novella Rael and Fred Rael (Daughter and Father)**

**Novella**

Growing up in a small, richly Hispanic community called

Questa, at times I would question my last name, Rael. I would sometimes wonder if Rael was the same as Israel, or are we from Israel? I thought of this, as I can recall, in high school. A name on my father's mother's side is Gómez. On my mother's mother's side there is the name of Espinoza.

When I moved from the small town in northern New Mexico, Questa, I met up with one of my classmates from this town. Her name is Carol. We became good friends. She met a woman from the southern part of New Mexico whose name I don't remember. Carol told the woman that she was from Questa and that her maiden name was Rael. She also mentioned that she had a good friend with the last name Rael. This woman told her that Rael is not a Spanish name, and the Raels come from Spain and are known as Spanish Jews. I was very intrigued by what Carol had told me. I really wasn't familiar with the Jewish religion and did not investigate any further. I did ask my father, Fred Rael, about our last name, but he really did not know much.

The only rituals, while I was growing up, that stand out in my mind are the women wearing black for one year (mourning for one year) after the death of a family member. The initial mourning period lasted for seven days, after which a prayer group would gather and pray for the deceased. People would visit during this seven-day period. We did have a two-day wake. A cross placed over the main entrance of the home was intended to keep evil spirits away.

During Easter, my mother would make this triangle-shaped dessert called *empanadas*. They would be filled with either pumpkin or prunes and were eaten during Christmas and Easter. We eat *panocha*, unleavened bread.

The chicken was killed in my family by the following method: It was grabbed by the neck and whirled around until it was decapitated. I remember the family talking about not eating pork after sunset. They would say it was too heavy.

I always felt that the Rael family was different. I would look at my father, and I noticed Daddy and his siblings did not really look like the typical dark-skinned Hispanics. I found out in high school that my father and the rest of his siblings went to private schools. At the time, only the children of families with money or big landowners would go to private schools. I asked my father about his schooling. He mentioned that his father always wanted a good education for his children.

I did ask Daddy where his family came from. His answer was Spain. I feel a connection to Judaism, especially because of the name.

**Guadalupe Ramos**

When I went to Rabbi Leon, I told him that there is no way I can prove I'm Jewish, no physical proof. The first thing I ever saw that was Jewish was a *Seder* for Passover. This was in a Protestant Church. I grew up Catholic. They had a special speaker who did the *Seder*. He explained the *Seder*, meaning of everything, and said he worked with elderly in Florida.

I thought we always say that God is the same, the God of Israel. At the *Seder*, I was wondering why the *Seder* is so different than anything celebrated in other faiths, Catholic and Protestant. If we worship the same God, why are we not all celebrating Passover the same way? I started to be interested in the Old Testament. That *Seder* was an awakening for me and brought a lot of questions. I started wondering about things that happened when I was pregnant with my son at the time of the *Seder*.

A few months later, I moved behind the Holocaust Museum in El Paso. The Jewish Community Center is behind my house. I had been meaning to go visit. One day, after shopping, I decided to stop by and go in. It was closed and a lady said they had a lot of things to offer there. They had Israeli dance classes, cooking, etc. I called a week later and went to a dance class. The strangest thing is that when they started playing the Israeli music, it was my favorite song, *Moreinu* (my teacher). I started to get a knot in my throat and didn't know why. I asked myself, "Why do I feel like this? Why am I so emotional here?" I couldn't talk or I might burst into tears. It was like that for six or seven months. I thought I might not go back. I kept going back, and it took about seven months to learn the dances. So that was my first encounter with Jewish people. Then there was an announcement on television for a Messianic Jewish place. I went and remember walking into a *Shabbat* service, and they were taking out a *Torah*. I had no idea what they were doing. I wanted to cry. A lady came and hugged me and said, "You have a Jewish heart and you're probably Jewish." I was there every Saturday. I thought, "She doesn't know what she's talking about." I'm Mexican. Mom is from Mexico. I was born in Fabens, Texas, forty-five minutes from El Paso. Father grew up there too. I kept going to the Messianic synagogue. Then this man told me, "You're probably Jewish. Did you notice a lot of Mexicans are Jews?" I thought that's strange. He said, "I see you here. I think you have a Jewish heart. I bet you have some Jewish blood in your background."

He gave me a book on crypto-Jews, descended from the Inquisition. It had last names and told how they were changed. I found my mother's last name, Guzmán, and Father's last name, Gutiérrez. Falcón and Castillo are names in his family. They were found in the book. I thought this incredible and thought now I'll talk to my mother. She said I was crazy. "We're not Jewish." My mother's history is sad. She was orphaned at eleven months and raised by a Catholic family. She was born in Jiménez, Chihuahua. She told me, "I don't know much about my family, and my father left for the United States to work and never returned (my Grandfather Guzmán)."

The thing is we grew up Catholic. I want to find out. I called my aunt, Father's sister, and asked if she could tell me anything about my background. She created a family tree on my father's side and went back to Galicia, Spain. She didn't know if we were Jewish. That's all the information I got. Maybe I'm nuts I thought. I started a support group for crypto-Jews at the Jewish Community Center. So that's how I met Rabbi Leon. We ate in the *sukkah* one day. I had seen a movie called *Song of the Sephardim*. It started when they were expelled from Spain and told of the places they settled. It told how the Sephardim had to hide their heritage and practice rituals in private. All these things didn't show me for sure that I was Jewish, but made me want to convert. I spoke to Rabbi Leon, explaining what I've been going through. My two daughters and my son converted. My husband didn't. He has been practicing Judaism for seven years and will eventually convert.

On 9/11, a miracle, my mother went to visit an old lady who grew up with her father. Her family helped my mother's grandmother (my great-grandmother) and her father (my grandfather), mother and son. They were talking about the horrible Twin Towers and kids not being sent home. My mother said, "My grandson, Lupe's son, was sent home when 911 happened." The lady said, "Why was he the only one?" My mother, Lupe, said, "He is only one of her children in a Jewish school, and the Jewish Community Center has kinder day school." (From there, the children would go to Hebrew day school.) The lady, Socorro, asked, "Why is he in a Jewish school?" My mother replied, "Didn't I ever tell you that my daughter converted to Judaism? She's Jewish." Socorro said, "Isn't it strange that your blood calls you back to your own blood?" My mother said, "What are you talking about?" Socorro responded, "Didn't they ever tell you that your father and grandmother were Jewish?" My mother said, "No, no one mentioned anything."

Lupe related Socorro's story:

One day my mother's grandmother came into the town's (Jiménez) main street, holding a little boy's hand (he was about four years old). They didn't know anyone. They went to Socorro's house asking for a place to stay and looking for work. Socorro's father gave them a room to stay in and helped them with food. My mother's grandmother started washing clothes and doing things for people so that they could survive. Socorro was little at the time, about seven, and she started visiting them a lot. She said she would see this lady light candles one day on the weekend, every weekend, and bake a bread. They would also eat this round bread, flat like a *tortilla*, only during Passover. During *Pasqua* (Passover) they ate this special unleavened bread. She would also tell Socorro's family to cover the mirrors when someone died. Socorro told Mother that my great-grandmother (Columba) swept toward the middle of the room. My youngest daughter does this just by herself.

Socorro said that when my Grandfather Guadalupe was seventeen years old, his mother was murdered. My mother asked why she was killed. She said because Great-Grandmother was Jewish. She didn't go to church or do anything the others did in town, a very small town. This was probably in the early 1900s. No one investigated anything. Socorro knew the reason. Nobody knew where my great-grandmother came from. Socorro only knew that they were Jewish. Mom never knew.

My mother called on September 11, with her voice breaking on the telephone, after visiting Socorro and said, "You're not that crazy after all." She said, "How did you know (meaning that we're Jewish)?" I said, "I didn't." This lady, Socorro, is still alive. I visited her and she said my youngest daughter looks like my grandfather (Mother's father).

Father died when I was seven. His family doesn't call us. We just have me, my brother, my mother, and that's our family. Father's father is from New Mexico. Grandmother is from Arizona. Father's sister has all this information from Galicia.

The lady that raised my mother called me *Judía-errante* (wandering Jew) when I was growing up. She never spoke of anything. She, Francisca Jordan, was a very good friend of my grandmother. That's why she raised my mother. Francisca never adopted my mother, and Mother did not know why.

When my Grandmother Francisca, the lady that raised my mother, passed away, nothing was given to us. Everything was given to Francisca's brothers and sisters.

## Henry Parra

I found that my family, the Parras, and on my maternal side, the Lópezes, came to New Mexico with the conquistador Don Francisco Vásquez de Coronado between 1540 and 1542. According to Guillermo Garmendia Leal's book, *Fundadores de Nueva Galicia,* which is research of the Archive of the Indies, included are Alonso Martín Parra, Alonso Rodríguez Parra, as well as about nine Lópezes, all being listed on Coronado's muster roll or list of participants who came along for the expedition. They came exploring, looking for gold and silver. That's why they came to New Mexico. Parras also came in 1598 with Don Juan de Oñate in the first colonizing expedition to New Mexico. According to George P. Hammond's *Don Juan de Oñate, Colonizer of New Mexico*, Gregorio Chacón Parra was a soldier with Oñate. Parras settled along the Rio Grande, with at least some going to Tome.

The thing was there might be a Sephardic link. In 1681, after the Spaniards had been chased out of New Mexico in 1680, Antonio de la Parra went to the area of Pueblo de San Antonio de Padua de Casas Grandes (probably to a place which became known as El Real De Corralitos), according to the research of Fray Angélico Chávez in *Origins of New Mexico Families*. I think my family was into mining and exploration. In 1682, the formal founding date of Pueblo de San Antonio de Padua de Casas Grandes, Antonio de la Parra was joined, perhaps upon notification of mineral discovery, by people from the village of Old Cerrillos in northern New Mexico which included the prominent family of Carvajals. Per old church records I have personally researched through the LDS Family Search Microfilms, our family seems to have intermarried with Carvajals. Carvajals were Jewish. I remember reading that a Carvajal was actually put to death by the Inquisition in Mexico City long ago. Similarly, Parras, Lópezes and most of my kin are families which were identified by the Catholic Church of Spain and the Inquisition to be of Jewish descent or suspect thus. Actual lists and related information can be read in Pere Bonnin's *Sangre Judía* or at http://www. sephardim.com.

I've learned all of this through my genealogical study. To this day, we have Carvajal relatives. These families were instrumental in founding the area because of mining. I think Parras, and some of our close kin such as Carvajales, Galindoses, Martínezes, Rodríguezes, and Valencias, to name a few, came together. We kind of stuck together. Families married within their own. As soon as Spaniards under De Vargas reconquered New Mexico from the Indians in 1692, many of the displaced families gradually moved back along the Rio Grande in New Mexico.

All these families came through Mexico. Eventually, my part of the family (Parras) moved to Dona Ana (Las Cruces Area). Then we migrated from there. We (a lot of kin or close people) would all go together. We wound up in Mimbres Valley, where our kin were amongst the original settlers. So that's where my father, Joaquín Galindo Parra, was born and raised. Later, the families separated some, especially after the Great Depression, going to California, etc. I was born in East Los Angeles. My father developed respiratory problems, and my own direct family returned to their New Mexico.

I recently received information/communication from another person's Parra family research. They had been doing archaeological and genealogical research at El Valle de San Buenaventura near the Casas Grandes area and found that there once existed a community of *conversos* or crypto-Jews there. The Parras and Carvajales, to name a few of my kin, were prominent in that area!

In 1680, Spaniards were chased out by the Indians. People continued to find a way to survive. My family, until the last century, was into mining. Grandfather had mining claims north of Deming in the Gila Forest, near their Mimbres ranch. Grandfather also had mining claims north of town here.

The family was always into exploration. They came from Spain through Extremadura. Before that they lived in Castile. I do not know if the eviction of Jews from Spain in 1492 pushed us on to the New World. The remoteness of New Mexico, however, was obviously good to get away from a Catholic Church intolerant of religious diversities and freedom and, of course, the Inquisition.

Growing up, the López family in my life leaned towards Protestantism. They avoided Catholicism. Mom's side came from El Valle de San Buena Ventura, near the Casa Grandes area, where I mentioned the existence of crypto-Jews. I was nonetheless baptized Catholic, as was my own mother who later joined her family in Protestantism. Somehow, because of their background, experiences, or traditions, you had to be baptized Catholic.

My father Joaquín was from an outwardly appearing Catholic family, though the men or Parras were not regular churchgoers. There is a strong faith in one God and that one God was everything fulfilling to them. Obviously, they married some women who took their Catholicism more devotedly, for some old *santos* (statuary of saints) from my ancestors still exist.

The elders from the Mimbres speak like the people from northern New Mexico, especially among themselves, because they've been here for so long, actually from the time of the Conquest. They can also understand and talk to the new Spanish-speaking immigrants, but like I said, amongst themselves you catch a trace of something different. Obviously, it is becoming lost. English was my first language, starting out my life away from the Mexican borderlands, and I was called a *pocho* (one of Hispanic heritage who does not speak Spanish correctly). Thus, I do not speak like they do, even though I have learned a lot of Spanish in my fifty-four years. Basically, they married Catholics. They're pretty well Catholic and somehow content with the knowledge that they were baptized. That seems to be enough for them. Except for new baptismal ceremonies and the occasional weddings, they are definitely not regular visitors to the places of worship. The family believed in circumcision.

The family slaughtered chickens by twirling them until they were decapitated. Then they placed them on a cross drawn in the earth. With sheep, they slit the neck, hung it up and drained the blood into the ground. It died peacefully. We don't eat blood. We didn't eat a lot of pork and beef, but venison—yes. Everybody in the family said, "There's one God." Up until my grandparent's generation, women stayed in bed a long time after giving birth. During Lent, my grandmas on both sides made unleavened bread—*galletas* which is kind of a generic term actually for biscuits or also for sugared cookies, which we called *biscochitos*. Fried bread topped with honey and called *bunuellos* (sic)—*buñuelos*— some places, but locally, *sopapillas*, were also enjoyed. We had *quelites* and *capirotada* during Lent.

Dad's side prayed too much according to elderly kin who loved to visit them, but the kids didn't like to go there to stay overnight or spend evenings with them because of so much praying. My dad kept everything to himself and prayed in Spanish. Dad followed Catholicism. The whole family prayed together, especially when I was young, although Mom was more Protestant. I wonder if we have Jewish blood, but I guess we won't know unless something like genealogical testing is done.

Mom, when we left to go on a trip, would have us gather and say a prayer. She would put her hands up. She was giving you a blessing. Actually, the whole family gathered. This is still done.

I wonder, "Are we accepted to go to our roots?" I'm confused about it. I want to know more. The Old Testament was important to my family. My mom had me read it. It was and remains my strength somehow.

I have begun a study of what Judaism is all about. I see that it is the foundation of Islam and Christianity. I am amazed at what I have learned thus far, including the belief that the gates to heaven are open to all good people, not just to any one religion. I have so much faith and belief in God, one and my only Great God. I have always prayed and looked to Him. It was and remains my strength somehow.

I am very moved by your visit to see me in a particularly special time for me. For about two years I have been reaching out to my ancestors or my heritage through genealogical study/research. I have found relatives, places, history, and information, which had already been forgotten. I have acquired and am reading Pere Bonnin's book, *Sangre Judía*. Another book by Seymour B. Liebman, *The Inquisitors and Jews in the New World,* is on the way.

As I said, it is quite amazing for me somehow. It all fits so well with everything IN my life, my beliefs, perhaps my soul. God wanted me to find this way!

### Hubert Jonathan Larribas (Brother of Frank N. Larribas)

I am Catholic now. Mom said that our ancestors were from Spain. There is a town in Spain with the name Larribas. Mother's name was Beatrice Torrez (maiden name). Mother was born in Magdalena, New Mexico. She married Nabor Larribas. Mother later divorced and remarried, and I had other brothers and sisters, half brothers and sisters. My grandmother, Mother's mother, was a Cedillo.

My great-uncle (Mother's uncle), A. A. Cedillo, was attorney general during Franklin D. Roosevelt's administration. His son was a general in the U.S. Army and a judge at the Nuremberg Trials in Germany. His name was Juan Sedillo. When the family came from Spain, the name was Cedillo.

The family was very secretive and never spoke of anything. My sister, Aleene, said that Mother put a *menorah* in the window for people to see when they came from other countries to work in the zinc and lead mines. Every Christmas, according to my sister, she put a *menorah* in the window to indicate our Jewish sympathies. My sister and brother both said that the *menorah* was the first thing up for Christmas and the last thing that came down. In Magdalena, they never called it a *menorah*. I found out what it was through books.

There was a one-year mourning period where the mourners were dressed in black. Mom wouldn't talk about anything Jewish because she married a very strict Catholic. She would sweep away from the door onto the patio. My brother, Colonel Chávez, said the family came to New Mexico because they could have been fleeing. We don't know. They didn't say anything about it in Magdalena because they were afraid.

The family believed in circumcision. Cutting the neck quickly killed animals. We hung animals to drain the blood. We did eat blood of animals. The family salted the meat of big animals and made jerky that they wanted to preserve. It would last for weeks. Mom made *buñuelos* for New Year's. We ate *panocha* and *capirotada* all the time. I made easy friends with Jewish people.

My real father, Larribas, said that his grandfather came here with the Spanish Armada from Spain looking for gold. I didn't know Father well. I believe that I have a Sephardic heritage from Spain because of the name and research of Jerry Martínez. He traces family heritage. Jerry Martínez went back to seventeen something, and he wrote the Larribas family tree in Albuquerque. He traced the Spanish heritage of my family (Larribas) back to 1540. He saw it in the records that Larribas was Spanish.

**James Abreu**

Santiago Abreu goes back to Spain. My name is James, and that is Santiago in Spanish. Santiago was a Spanish soldier, and I got the information from a Dr. Joseph Sánchez. He's the director of the Spanish Colonial Research Center in New Mexico. His secretary is Edwina Abreu, and she's married to an Alfred Abreu. We just discovered that they are cousins. A Connie Abreu called and said that we're cousins.

Joseph Sánchez has done research. He has gone to Spain and Mexico and has documentation of Spanish military records. They sailed from Cadiz and went to the Canary Islands. From there, they went to Cuba, Vera Cruz, Mexico City, Texas, and Santa Fe. He came here in the mid 1700s, probably somewhere between 1780 and 1785. Those are the first records of Abreus in New Mexico. The family stayed in New Mexico. I think Santiago's son was the governor of New Mexico around 1833. His name was also Santiago. There were brothers by the name of Marcelino Abreu and Ramón. They were killed in the Revolution of 1837 along with the governor.

The governor was Alvino Pérez from Mexico. He was aristocratic and still had the Spanish trappings. He distanced himself from the peasants. He got them very upset with him and his administration. Ramón was a judge in that administration. Santiago was a mayor of Santa Fe. I think Marcelino was a school superintendent and a schoolteacher. Santiago's son, Jesús, was my great-great-grandfather. He was born in 1823 and died in 1900. My dad was Ernie. My grandfather was Ernest. His father was Ramón, and Ramón's father was Jesús. Jesús' father was Santiago. This is the lineage through the Abreus. Charles Beaubien (French) was the father of Jesús' wife.

Jesús bought a 30,000 acre ranch in northern New Mexico, around 1859, from a Spaniard by the name of Joseph Clay. Jesús' wife, Petra Beaubien, was his goddaughter. She was his favorite, and he offered his ranch to Jesús and Petra. So they bought it from him. That was a family compound. In effect, it was a small village, and it was called Rayado. People married within the compound. My grandfather was born in Rayado. There was an Ashkenazi influence in that area from the traders.

There are many Abreus in Portugal and in Brazil. There is a village in northern Spain with the name Abreu. Santiago's father was Yante and he was from Catalonia. That's as far back as I have gone on the Abreu side. I still have to talk to Dr. Sánchez to see if he knows more.

My mother's side was Wildenstein. My grandmother was Quintana Ortega, and she married a Wildenstein, an Ashkenazi Jew. My grandmother is the one who spoke only Spanish. In her home, the curtains were drawn. It was always dark in the house. She was always in the kitchen. The windows in the kitchen would be open, and the curtains were drawn in the back of the house. She covered her head every time she went out of the house. She died when she was ninety-eight. The house was full of religious pictures and statues, the Catholic stuff. There was a certain time when my great-grandmother would wash her hair. I think she would sweep away from the door.

After birth, the mother would not wash for thirty days. We would place a piece of coral on the baby's shoe to ward off evil spirits. Mother made me do this with our children. We had cats, and she didn't want us to keep cats with the babies. They might suck the breath out of the babies.

I always had the feeling that you don't talk to neighbors or share a lot. You would stay within your own group. Older people had friends, but they didn't reveal much to them. My great-grandmother, who spoke only Spanish, and her daughter, Jane, my mother's mother, was always saying, "You don't talk to the neighbors about your family." They were secretive. It was kind of what's in the house stays in the house. Keep family secrets.

Father's mother, Eva Olona, had a Spanish name. Her mother was a Mascarenas, her mother's maiden name. That's a place in Spain that has to do with masks. Spaniards, with a Jewish heritage, often took the names of places where they lived when leaving Spain. I feel comfortable with Judaism.

## Jo Roybal Izay

Jewish families fled Spain and scattered worldwide. My ancestors fled Spain, went to Portugal, then to the Canaries, and made their way to the New World. Hoping to find a better life away from the dangers of an Inquisition, they landed in New Mexico and remained prisoners of nomadic Indians for over two hundred years. Land grants were issued to the colonizers, and they took advantage of them.

Colonization of New Mexico began in 1598. Most of them were *conversos*. In those days that meant nothing. It left the people free to worship as they saw fit. Those who lived in the lowlands had limited religious direction—very limited. Spain's main concern was to Christianize the heathen Indians. All New Mexicans shared the same traditions and with the passing of time, they forgot the reasons why. Survival was their only concern.

Neither Spain nor New Spain (Mexico) gave the colonizers protection, provisions, munitions, doctors, dentists, schools— nothing.  These forgotten people were left to fend for themselves.  As I look back, I can see why.  Being born Jewish was not a big surprise for me as it has been to many New Mexicans.  I knew it all along.  My grandfather made sure that we knew about our roots.  We worshiped the God of Israel, *Adonai*.  The Sephardic Jews were expecting their Messiah to be born in New Mexico, but alas, it didn't happen and eventually they all came to accept Jesus as the Messiah.

Perhaps having been isolated in the wilderness of the Sangre de Cristo Mountains in northern New Mexico had a lot to do with our way of life, which was totally different from people living in the lowlands.  My ancestors founded the village where I was born in 1785.  The place is more beautiful than anyone can imagine.  It's like a kingdom in the wilderness. Alas, for my ancestors, it was a miserable kingdom.

Owning land meant little in those early days.  Pueblo Indians and Spanish families formed an alliance and protected each other from the ravishing raids that left them unable to make progress in their new surroundings.  They would build their homes only to have them burned to the ground. Generation after generation found people regressing not only in traditions, but in language as well.  Poverty, disease, and misery took over.

Many Jews brought bags of gold that they had mined in Zacatecas, New Spain, hoping to build great cities and universities in New Mexico.  They so wanted to rebuild the lives they had in Spain.  According to legend, the gold remained buried in the vast wilderness where the people remained trapped.  Their hopes and dreams vanished.  They were hopeless and helpless.  They were forgotten by the outside world.  The poor souls were known only to those living among them, and lived and died with no one to record their suffering.

Men, women, and children toiled the land only to have the

nomads raid, steal and burn, kidnap and kill as soon as everything was done. Men traveled in groups to Taos or Santa Fe to trade. Sometimes they would make it back to their homes intact; other times they were found dead. Their suffering subsided when New Mexico became a territory of the United States in 1846.

In 1850, the infamous Archbishop Lamy took over the diocese. The first thing he did was to excommunicate Spanish priests and raise havoc with the Penitentes, a religious sect. Jews feared a *gringo* inquisition and joined the Catholic Church in droves. Others, like my ancestors who felt they had to live a separated life, joined the Presbyterian Church in order to read their Bibles openly and without prejudice. In reality, they went underground because there was a lack of Presbyterian ministers and it was perfect for them.

It has been somewhat of a shock to me to find that there is an interest in New Mexico's Sephardic roots. There are those who will argue that we are "wannabes." To those I say, I am perfectly happy with who I am and don't want to be like other Jews. I am proud of my heritage and maintain many of the Sephardic traditions. I neither envy nor do I care to emulate anyone. I speak Ladino, standard Spanish, and English.

The most important thing to me is that my ancestors helped pave the way to the greatest state of the Union, New Mexico, and the Land of Enchantment. I value everything that I am and all that I learned from my grandfather who made sure that we knew who we were. Our New Mexico traditions are unlike those in other parts of the world. They may not resemble traditions in other parts of the world, and that's all right. We are who we are and love who we are. *Shalom.*

**Lorenzo Domínguez**

I realized my Jewish heritage, in full, about five to six years ago, after always having unanswered questions. My older sister, the oldest in the entire family, always believed we were Jewish and told me that. I also realized that we had a Jewish heritage because of the dialect of Spanish we spoke, which I found out was Ladino.

My grandmother would always drink a little glass of Mogen David on Friday nights and never cook pork. We would eat *quelites* which is a wild spinach grown in New Mexico. We ate this during *Pesach*, Passover, as the bitter herbs.

My great-grandmother's family was a very quiet group who did not practice many Catholic rituals. She also handed down to my mother a Jewish prayer shawl that my mother still has today.

I always felt different from everyone else growing up in

Catholic schools. I asked too many questions and always questioned if Jesús was really the Messiah. This, of course, got me into a lot of trouble. Eventually, my parents took me out of Catholic schools. For many years, I remained in limbo, not knowing in which direction to go.

Finally, tracing my grandmother's family back to a province in Spain, did I come to the conclusion that we were descendants of the Jews of Spain—expelled, tortured, and murdered for many years. Many of my ancestors were tried during the Mexican Inquisition, and fortunately were able to escape here to New Mexico where my family goes back nine generations.

My return to Judaism has been a wonderful awakening, and I feel a deep closeness and understanding to all Jewish people. I cherish the Jewish faith and practices and know, deep in my heart, that I, Levi ben Macario—my Hebrew name—have returned home.

**María Apodaca**

**COMING HOME** (Speech Upon Return to Judaism)

My name is Meirah bat Shlomo Elisheva (I am the daughter of Solomon and Ella) which comes from a translation of my middle name Clarita, given to me in honor of my grandmother. Clare means "to cast light upon" or "to light up." Today, I feel that light burning in my heart for I have found a home in Judaism.

For years, I have had a burning need to discover the history of my ancestry. In pursuing this, I learned that I am a descendant of the Sephardic Jews of Spain that survived the Spanish Inquisition. They came to the New World for freedom, but continued to keep the true identity of their religion a secret. As a teenager in high school, we were studying the five great religions of the world. I chose to write about Judaism. After my father reviewed my work, he slowly put the paper down and told me something that I would have never guessed on my own. He told me this in a very secretive way. The three little words that my father used changed my life forever: "We were Jews."

For years, I have been searching for information about this history. It has been a difficult task, but I have had some important success. This past year, I learned that my great-grandmother, Petritia Chávez-Luna, was a practicing Jew. She, her brother, and sister-in-law would get together on Saturdays and were not to be disturbed. Great-Uncle Clemente even had a *menorah* in his home. I had no idea that my roots to Judaism were so close. I thank my family and friends for their support. (*Cuedo decar que tengo mucho olguio a desar que soy Heja de Israel.*) I can say that I am very proud to be a daughter of Israel. I am happy that I come from a very strong and brave people.

**María D. Sánchez**

My family has been in New Mexico for hundreds of years.

When I began traveling outside of New Mexico I started realizing we didn't do things like other Catholics. I just pondered for a long time. I was going to travel to China with a friend of mine. Mom wanted me to go to Israel (the family kind of pitched in for me to go). I went to Israel and started noticing that everyone in Israel had manners and behaviors like we did. I didn't have any problems and was accepted everywhere. Our body language, ways of looking at things, and hospitality were similar. I noticed all these things that were similar to the Sephardim and felt as though I hadn't left Albuquerque.

As I was praying, I opened scripture to the Book of Zephaniah, Chapter 3, Verses 14 through 20. I thought something was weird. It was so easy for me to walk into places, and feel as though I was accepted as a *sabra*. Even when I spoke Spanish there, it was fine. One of the main rabbis in Israel was a *Toledano*. He was the Sephardic Chief Rabbi. The Sephardim would take the names of the cities from which they came after the expulsion. The Book of Zephaniah is found with the Minor Prophets. Part of the scripture is about the gathering of the scattered Israelites. It says, "I will dance over you and renew you in my love." The Sephardim here are very spiritual. And so I came out and asked the pastor who was leading the tour, "Are there Jews that are Spanish?" She said, "Yes, they're Sephardic." I felt that God was guiding me.

When I came home, my grandmother was waiting for me at the airport. A few days later, I asked her if we were Jews. She said, "*Somos Israelitas* (we are Israelites)." Our people are content living and practicing Judaism without advertising it. It is a way of life where you are taught to do certain things. Grandma would say, "When God divided, God scattered." This was in reference to Roman times, when Jews were scattered into Europe and Sefared.

A documentary is in progress about my Sephardic family history. Fay Blake introduced me to Loggie Carrasco and she is a cousin on both sides. My mother went to school with her, but I had never met her. We discussed many things. She's helped a lot of our people and is a very giving person. Sephardic families protect each other. When we don't want anyone in, we don't let them in. There is a very close bond within the family. Distant cousins used to marry distant cousins—fourth cousins. This is still done to some degree. This was done basically to keep the secrecy and for protection because they didn't want outsiders reporting on their Jewish practices.

The documentary includes proverbs traced to the Sephardim in Turkey. My grandmother, when I was young, would get me up early in the morning and talk about God, to know Him vs. to knowing about Him. It wasn't a religious thing. For us, it's a relationship.

In the evening, Grandfather would be reciting the prayers. Some of these prayers were a combination of Catholicism and Judaism. We just had certain times we would pray. It was very normal for us to do what we were doing, so I never suspected anything about Judaism or that anything was different.

We had a forty-one day wait after a child was born. You keep kosher and keep certain foods that you eat. Basically, there was no sexual activity. It was a cleansing period, a restorative period, a time of prayer, and a time of spirituality. Women would have to use certain herbs.

Great-Grandma, on Father's side, was a healer who died at 110 years of age. Her husband was 125 when he died. She led all the grandkids around the house praying. She got dirt from the ground and spread it on the blanket and on the pillow, both of which were outside the house. She had one grandkid go get the pillow and the blanket for her. She knew she was dying. She was in a sitting position when she gave her blessing to the grandkids, telling the eldest grandchild to take care of them all. She just lay down and died. People around here just know things. My grandma and grandpa would bless you when you were getting married, going to school, going on a trip, or before death. I got lots of those. That was pretty normal, and that's what was done in the family.

Before Grandma died, she started to remove luxuries, vanities, and flowers and asked one grandchild to cover the mirrors. Grandpa placed a cap outside on the fence to let people know that this was a house of mourning. Grandma was a Toledo. We had food brought into the house. During the wake, two people were chosen by the family to guard the body and pray for the body—the soul. They prayed all night. This was done during Grandma's early years. We threw soil onto the coffin and still do it. Also, we place a stone at the grave site. A rabbi explained that Great-Grandmother, on Father's side, threw dirt on the pillow and blanket because, according to research, the Sephardim couldn't get back to

Israel. They would either get dirt from Israel and throw it into the coffin or they would drill holes in the bottom of the coffin because they would try to be close to the earth.

Today, there is a year waiting period before setting the headstone. We place stones on headstones to show that we were there. Prayers indicated that there is only one God and were combined with Catholicism. We used *Dio* (God) and *Dios* (Gods) in the family.

People here were Kabbalistic. In Kabbala there is something about the Trinity according to an author by the name of Gershon. Acceptance of these beliefs is easy for Sephardim because they live by the spirit of the law rather than the letter of the law. You have to be kind of a rabbi to understand the people here.

We avoided blood. Although we ate some pork, it was frowned upon. It was considered dirty.

I took Spanish all through school, but where I lucked out was that most of the Spanish teachers were from this area. They let me slide because they spoke the same Spanish. I remember in high school one teacher spoke Castilian Spanish. He said, "You're going to have to learn your Spanish all over again." I became so angry that I transferred out of his class. At that time I didn't understand. Now that I have heard Ladino, and I am a mental health therapist working with people from Mexico, I automatically know their roots. Most people today do not speak Ladino; they speak English. Ladino is dying out with our parents. Speaking to Rabbi Lynn, I thought maybe we can start teaching it to the kids.

I've never been asked to attend a welcoming-back ceremony. How can I be welcomed back when I never left? Our people did our best to keep what we have. As for becoming a rabbi, I was talking to Rabbi Lynn. Since my mid-twenties, I felt guided. I've been doing the Sephardic sermons in Nahalat Shalom. Rabbi Lynn and Rabbi Celnick are mentoring me.

Three rabbis will come in on my ordination as a rabbi. Rabbi Celnick is a very good friend of the family. He did the blessings for my grandparents and father before they died. God bless him! Rabbi Lynn has known my family for a long time.

I'm also looking into the Reconstructionist movement. I'm not too concerned with what people think about, just concerned with what my people need spiritually, with the understanding and preservation of their history. The people are important. People find out that they are Sephardic and don't know where to go.

When Grandma was slaughtering animals, she would explain, "This is what you eat; this is what you don't eat." Blood drained into the earth and was then covered with the earth. We twirled chickens until they were decapitated. We don't eat red meat.

On the Day of John the Baptiste, *El Día de San Juan*, we would bathe in moving water. It was like a purification. The family went in as a whole. No other Catholics practiced this.

When a baby was ill, we would put a *sanbenito* on him. A *sanbenito* was condemned garb during the Inquisition. This goes back to asking the martyrs to intercede for this child who is ill.

We learned Catholic prayers, but most important were the Ten Commandments in my home. It is important for me that people know there will be a place, here in New Mexico, where descendants of Sephardim can inquire about their heritage, a place where they can keep in touch so that we don't lose so many. I want people to understand—Yes, there will be a rabbi here, someone whom people can contact. Because we're doing this through Temple Nahalat Shalom, the congregation will help them find me to welcome them and accept them. I have already started with Nahalat Shalom, as a sister synagogue to us—to establish something of a haven where Sephardim can meet, Catholic or not.

**María Emilia Martínez**

I realized that I had a Jewish connection after being a part of my cousin's Jewish wedding. I then began to question an actual heritage after reading a book written by an Orthodox Rabbi. I discovered traditions and customs that paralleled Jewish tradition. At this point, I began to ask my grandmother and mother questions regarding the origins of these parallel traditions. Later, I attended a *Yom Kippur* service and left elated. I finally knew that I was home and whole. Most of this discovery occurred in my late twenties.

My grandmother lit candles on Friday nights. She told me that it was a Catholic tradition. Yet, she also prepared kosher dishes, and my grandfather followed *kashrut* practices in butchering the cows and chickens on their farm. They covered mirrors when someone passed away and placed stones on the graves of family members. Many families in the Pecos, New Mexico, area also had mourning practices similar to

Jewish tradition. Also, my grandmother made sure that she cooked on Friday so that she rested on Saturday.

I feel a deep connection to Judaism. I now know that I am Jewish. I feel that God has revealed to me my true identity. My mother recently visited Spain, and a historian told her that our family from the Valencia province is indeed Jewish. I am becoming more whole as I study and practice Jewish traditions. Hopefully, I will make my *bat mitzvah*. This would probably be the first in my lineage. I also hope that my son will someday *bar mitzvah*. He is only two and a half. Yet he is fully aware that we celebrate *Shabbat*. I will bring him up teaching him that he is a Sephardic Jew.

**Dr. Maurilio Vigil**

It was understood in the family, always just said that, "You are Hispanic," that "Your ancestors were from Spain." The name was a significant thing to my father and me. It's something that he always said. "You have to protect your name. You always have to honor your name. It is something that always follows you wherever you go, for good or bad." It was always stressed, "Take pride in your name and your heritage." That heritage also includes your Catholic heritage. He was religious. He was a Catholic and a Penitente. My original family surname was actually Montes Vigil.

We discovered that the first Vigil came here in 1611. Our ancestor was Juan Montes Vigil. We made a definitive connection with Juan Montes Vigil. Prior to my research, my family had very little knowledge of these ancestors. These are things I discovered from genealogical research in Sevilla's Archives of the Indies, where they have all the records of all the people who came from Spain to the New World. All of this area was called the Indies, *Indias* in Spain, at that time. They refer to *contrataciones* or contracts there. These people entered into a contract with the monarch to gain permission to come to the New World. I found our ancestor's name there. That's where I found Juan Montes.

All of these people had to prove that they were *sin mancha*, without any taint (without traces of Jewish blood) and that they were very strong Catholics. They had to show it very definitively. A person had to go through a lot of examination. For some reason, Juan Montes' parents had died, and he had to be sponsored by his uncle who happened to be the equivalent of a city councilor in the community. He had to testify that he (Juan Montes Vigil) came from a family of strong Catholics, with a strong military tradition of serving The Crown. The authorities were very explicit that there could not be a Jewish connection. This may have been a formality, but it was a formality they did follow strictly. If it's a formality, why did they need people to testify on their behalf? Montes Vigil had all kinds of people testify as to his character. Juan Montes Vigil was not wealthy. He had to find a sponsor, and a man by the name of Jacinto de Olmos sponsored him. Vigil was classified as a *criado* (servant). Juan was originally from San

Martín de Siero but was living in Madrid at the time of his application to come to the New World. All records for all *pasajeros* (passengers), as we said above, are in the Archivo de Las Indias (in Sevilla). They are in a building that's completely separated, and it's only for that purpose. Most American historians who want to do genealogy go there.

I would say that in some cases, the rituals practiced could be Sephardic. There were Spanish Jews (Sephardim) who came to the New World and went underground because of the Inquisition, but they maintained some of their customs. In New Mexico, there was not a lot of social interaction between the Ashkenazi Jewish merchants and the *Hispano* population. Therefore, there wasn't much influence from the Ashkenazi Jews upon the *conversos*. It depended when they came. The first Jews, coming as merchants, might have interacted because they may have been the only Jews in the community. In order to survive, they would have to socialize with the Hispanic community. In some cases their children might have intermarried with Hispanic families, depending how orthodox they were.

Later on, as more Jews came in the 1800s, they came in groups or families. There was a Jewish community already here, and they interacted with that community socially and religiously. These were people who were of a different class, more affluent. They were merchants. Chances are, if they interacted with anyone outside the Jewish community, it was with what we call here in New Mexico—Anglos. They were business people. In other words, in my view, Sephardic Jewish influences may have affected *Hispano* customs and culture, despite suppression by the Inquisition. We know that Sephardim secretly practiced their rituals, even though they were formally forbidden. They were passed on to their descendants without explanation. Later, other *Hispanos* could have emulated, picked up the same customs. The later Jewish merchants (Ashkenazim) who came to the Southwest generally kept customs in their own community—socially and religiously. Although they sold goods to the *Hispano*s, they did not intermarry as often so that their influence on the Hispanic culture was not as direct.

When killing goats, my family cut the jugular, and then hung the animal to drain the blood. My parents believed in circumcision, but I'm not sure they did it. We would light candles for the dead. Mom would light small candles in a glass too. The picture of a saint would be on the glass. Candles were lit in the bedroom. I did it myself.

We would sweep away from the door. My wife does this. A lot of the Jewish people who came to New Mexico, European merchants (Jewish or not), were mostly Ellis Island people. They went down to St. Louis. St. Louis was the main point of embarkation for New Mexico merchants. Earlier, before the railroad, French Canadians came down the Mississippi from Canada. We have a lot of French Canadian influence in New Mexico. These were people that came in as fur traders and trappers with a "Kit Carson" type background.

My family came from Pecos, which is between here and Santa Fe. There was an inclination to marry people within the community. It was a small village. I was told that we spoke a different Spanish in New Mexico. We were told this by people from Latin American countries. We're also told this by people from Mexico. "The Spanish you speak here is different." We know that. It could have had a Ladino influence. We call it an archaic form of Spanish, the Spanish most commonly spoken in Spain in the seventeenth and eighteenth century. A lot of the people who came from Spain to New Spain didn't spend a lot of time in Mexico. They came up to the frontier and had little contact with the evolving language in Mexico. Juan Montes, Jr. was born in New Spain. He had a son Francisco Montes who was the first Vigil who came to Santa Fe around 1690.

Even when the family moved to Las Vegas, my father would go back to the Pecos chapter of the Penitentes every weekend, especially during the Lenten period. He wanted to make sure there were enough people to participate in the ceremonies. They would spend all day Sunday there. They would call each other brothers, *hermanos*. There were several hundred chapters of the Penitentes. Each chapter had its own *morada*. It's a Spanish word. House of Worship is a common term used for all the *moradas*. The Penitentes were widespread in New Mexico and in southern Colorado. There are basic similarities and some differences. In the 1920s there was an effort on their part to organize into a formal hierarchical organization. Archbishop Lamy, who came to New Mexico approximately in 1850, was very critical of the Penitentes and disavowed them. He attacked their practices, flagellation and torture people would undergo in their worship rituals. He said this was against the Catholic religion. The Penitentes then went underground.

Lamy wanted to change everything and caused resentment. There was much friction between him and the native clergy. He ended up excommunicating some of the most prominent priests. The Spanish priests pretty much tolerated the Penitentes. The *morada* was usually outside the village. They would call themselves, for example, the *Morada of San José*, meaning the chapter of San José. Although the name of the chapel itself was also *morada*, my father belonged to the *Morada of Pecos*. Father knew of a *morada* outside of town in Sheridan. I asked him why he didn't go to that one. He would go instead to Pecos because he didn't like that one. He felt at home in his chapter. His relatives were part of that chapter. When he died, we took him back there. They performed a *velorio* (wake) and rosary for him as part of the burial ceremony.

In those days, there were very few avenues of education, so the church was a source of education. The church offered a good means of education. Studying for the priesthood and entering the military were means of getting an education. There was not much of a public education system. Thus, the church's influence was also transmitted through the educational process. There was a concern about the Masons when Lamy came in. There were other kinds of secret organizations, not all religious. Here in Las Vegas, we had the Society of St. Joseph. To commemorate their hundred-year celebration, they asked me to write an article for the newspapers to publicize their celebration and lent me their minutes. While reading these minutes (they had the minutes from the time the organization was founded, around 1873), I recall that in the minutes, the founding principles (the bylaws), it said to guard against influences of groups such as the secret Masons. That was one of the purposes of founding this religious organization. This San Jose Society was contrary to the Penitentes who were shunned by the church. The society was embraced by the church.

The church was kind of saying, "We want an alternative to the Penitentes," guarding against subversive influences of groups like the Masons who they feared would have an influence in trying to convert some of the Hispanic population. It was a Hispanic organization. The St. Joseph Society was encouraged and embraced by the bishop. The bishops said, "We encourage you because, one, you are not going to do the bad things that the Penitentes do. Secondly, we do need this kind of organization." I remember mentioning the Masons, the secretive organizations, and the influences they might have on the population. That's kind of related to what you are talking about, the church telling people not to practice Jewish customs. The higher-up clergy, priests and bishops, may have suspected that there were some customs practiced by the church, or some influences that the Masons were trying to prevail upon the Hispanic population. They viewed the Society of St. Joseph as being helpful to prevent that.

I did not avoid church. We were very active in the church. My mother lit candles for special occasions, not necessarily Friday night. She had her favorite statues of saints, and she would light candles to them for different purposes. Each saint had a different purpose, like St. Jude for troubled times or special needs. There are Esters in my family.

The Penitentes conducted services. Certain hymns, *canticos*, would be sung by the *hermanos* (Penitentes) during the wake. These hymns would also be sung during Holy Week, during the culmination of Lent. They would have meetings of the *morada* every first Sunday of the month. They would have rituals performed, take care of business, prayers, and initiation of new members. They would have ceremonies. If a member was sick, there was a member known as an *enfermero* (nurse). That person was responsible for going over and taking care of the sick person, literally being a nursemaid to him. Then there was another person responsible for making sure the family was taken care of. This man would go out and see if there was enough food at home. If a member was ill and wasn't working, they would collect money and make sure the chores were done, getting firewood, etc.

When a person died, the ritual was that the brotherhood would take over. They would arrange everything, wake and burial, in the traditional village. They would conduct a rosary and prayers as part of the wake. They would continue to take care of the family after burial for a reasonable period of time, to get them over the mourning. Part of the obligation of *hermanos* (Penitentes), although it is rare today, was to have an all-night wake. Burial is usually within twenty-four hours. The bereaved would sit in his house for a few days. People would visit and bring food. There was a one-year mourning period. The grave is sometimes marked with stones. Stones are used as markers, as borders, to show where the person is buried.

There are a lot of things done in the Catholic Church, in New Mexico today, that are not done in any other part of the country, probably a reflection of other religions. Still, today, in some families, for a son to choose priesthood is truly an honor. It's stronger here than in other parts of country. It's a tradition, some kind of blessing to the family.

If I discovered that I had Jewish ancestry, it wouldn't make a difference. It would just add to my identity. While I may practice some customs that may have Jewish origins, I am not aware of them. I was raised as a Catholic, by strong Catholics, and that is still my church. But, being an objective person, I can see the value and influence of other religions in our lives.

### Michele Greene

Greene is my father's name. He was Irish, and his grandparents were from Ireland. Mom's father, Robert Norton, was from Virginia, and he met my grandmother in Mexico. Greene is a name from my father's side.

My mother was Rosa Norton Luna. Her mother, my grandmother, was María Eloisa Dickson-Luna. The name had been de Luna until her grandmother's time. We have Sephardic heritage from Aragon. The family left Spain a few years after the expulsion in 1492; they were probably crypto-Jews. When I was growing up, I went to Catholic school because of Father's dominant family life. The reason why I was so influenced by that was because his huge Irish Catholic family lived in the northeastern United States—Boston, Rhode Island, and the New York area. I had a lot more interrelation and contact with them. I was raised in Washington, D.C. Both parents had come there to work during the war, my father from Rhode Island and my mother from El Paso. Mom was born in El Paso. Her family came from Chihuahua.

I was told I was Jewish while living in Washington, D.C. Living in Washington, I never thought any other family in the world practiced rituals such as me. My parents met during the war working in Washington and had four of us. I'm the youngest. Because there weren't a lot of Hispanics at that time in the D.C. area, my mother felt pressured to assimilate and be like all Americans. She wanted to blend in. Her family was pale skinned and it was easy. Father's family was prejudiced against anyone not Irish Catholic. Mother didn't bring up her background and blended in with the environment.

Mom's mother had to work because she was widowed at twenty-three, but her grandmother raised my mother and her one sister. She taught them a rigid form of Catholicism. They went to mass and were very observant. Her grandmother cooked for the priest. At the same time, she knew the Old Testament extremely well. One reason she cooked for the priest was to gain access to his books. They lived next door to the parish.

They were very poor when my grandmother and great-grandmother came to El Paso in 1915 (Mexican Revolution related). There was a big influx of Chihuahua people to the border because they were killing (rich!) people in Mexico. Their land was taken away. Grandmother was widowed and worked. My mother and her sister were born here in El Paso. My great-grandmother raised Mother and her sister. They used to really emphasize appearance as being well behaved. This still trickles down. That is partly a Chihuahua thing. Never tell your troubles. Everything has to be perfect. You had to keep you mouth shut and not make waves. Appearances on every angle, including manners and the Catholic thing such as saying the rosary in public counted a lot. Public display of devotion to Catholicism was important. This still exists within the family, especially with one of my brothers. He's like the ultimate pillar of the rigid Catholic Church. He follows Catholicism to the letter of the law and believes it, I need to stress. It isn't just show with him. My mother grew up really well-schooled.

My great-grandmother knew a lot of *Talmudic* and rabbinic stuff. The family of my great-grandmother were definitely practicing Jews. Great-Grandmother Trinidad, nicknamed Mimi (de Luna Hernández), I think, was born Jewish and might have been a practicing Jew. From what I'm trying to gather, maybe she was concerned for her safety as she converted or didn't call attention to her Judaism. She was born in 1856. The Inquisition had only ended recently. She knew you should not call attention Judaically. Judaism was very strong with her. When I was little, Mom would tell me stories of her Grandmother Mimi. My mom bonded with her. She was her biggest influence. She fed my mother knowledge and information about the Bible. My mother was like a scholar herself. My aunt wasn't interested and didn't care about school or religion either (the show of going to church, etc., yes, but the spirituality, no!) When I was little, I liked that too.

My oldest brother and I liked studying religion. Since I was very little, my mother gave me a Hebrew alphabet book and Jewish children's books. They progressed as age appropriate. Even though I was going to Catholic schools, she was giving me all these Jewish things, lots of books. As a child, you don't know that's strange.

I never felt a conflict with Catholic school until the third grade. I never spoke of anything; it's just what Mom did. Mom never set it up like a conflict. It's just what we did. In the third grade, we had a teacher, a crazy nun, obsessed with communism, occasionally poll us. One day she said, "If you were standing in the street and this communist came up and asked, 'If you weren't a Catholic what would you be?'" I said very innocently, "I'd ask him if I could be a Jew." You were supposed to be a martyr and say, "I would die for my faith." She couldn't understand and got really angry, I must stress. How could I say that? Where did it come from? I was upset, went home and cried. She called my mother. Mother was angry at her. I was crying. Mother then told me, "If they ever say anything about Jews, I want you to tell me immediately. Don't let them talk badly about Jews, and don't ever let them force you to choose." I got confused. I was eight. I said, "I don't know what I'm supposed to do now." I thought, "Was she telling me that I don't have to be a Catholic?" She said, "Oh, yes! Always act like a Catholic." Then I thought to myself. That's the first time I realized that there was something more, but my mom is the ultimate Catholic. Thinking, "How can she be so flexible about emphasizing not to insult the Jews?" I didn't know what that meant. I responded and followed her instructions, but I didn't know why.

Another time in school, they started talking about how wonderful that the church had managed to wipe out all the infidels. I thought it was wonderful to destroy the enemy of all that is right and good. I thought these people deserved to be wiped out. I thought the infidels were the enemy of the people, that they were evil. I asked my mother, "Did you know that the church killed all the infidels?" She said, "Who told you that?" I was upset and confused. "When you don't understand a word, look it up in the dictionary." My mother always told us, made us, look up unknown words in the dictionary. (The infidels were the people who were Moors or Jewish. Infidels were anyone who was not in the church.)

We had to go to confession every Friday and church regularly. It was so emphasized in the family. Father, who was so "Catholic," was lax about going to confession, not church. My father said, "I wouldn't go. Don't make her go if she's so scared." He didn't want to reveal his private life to anyone, but Mom said we had to go. So I went to confession, and once the priest was yelling at me. I went home upset and thought my mother would take his side. Instead, she sided with me and said, "Why are you paying any attention to what the priests say in confession? You have to go to confession, but just ignore them." This literally shook me up. I'd always been sure my mother was the ultimate enforcer of Catholic doctrine. I thought she was so devout, pillar of our church. (And indeed that is still how all her Catholic friends see her.) In the meantime, she was giving me Jewish books. I remember her giving me the Chaim Potok novels such as *The Chosen*. She also gave me a book called *Explaining Judaism to Christians and Jews*. Then my brother, Kevin, would say, "Why are you always giving her Jewish books? Why is she writing Hebrew letters?" I then realized that all of my siblings were not all doing the same things. I just thought that at a certain age we were all doing the same things.

When I was about twelve, my mother came into my bedroom with a packet of goodies, a *Haggadah*, a very beautiful hand-crocheted *kippah*, and a brass *Hanukkiah* from Turkey. David Gitlitz, as a favor to me, had the fibers of the *kippah* typed to try and verify the period of these religious items and found out they were probably Moroccan, definitely North African, at least one hundred twenty years old. I found out, half told and half verified, that the family lived in Morocco where they practiced Judaism before they came here. Mom said, "These were in the family forever because they were Jews." They were ritually handed down to one child in each generation, and she was glad that she had me last because she always knew that I was "the Jewish one." Even when I was little, I had such an affinity and such a response to Judaism.

My older brother, Bob, was the eclectic one. He was a Unitarian, an Episcopalian, and other things too. He is very embracing of our past. He's very supportive of me. He considers himself Jewish genealogically, but he doesn't practice. He has no problem with that. There was an emphasis on him to become a priest; but he also willingly wanted to go ahead and be a Jesuit, since he is a spiritual guy and an intellectual, both traits of being a Jesuit. Mom pushed him and he did start the Jesuit seminary. He almost got ordained but left (asked to leave) over the birth control issue. He was for it and wrote/spoke out against the pope banning it. He was too liberal even for a Jesuit. When he lived in Atlanta, he had taken me to a rabbinical conference, and he will sit with me here in the synagogue in El Paso. He met his wife when they were both Unitarians. She's a social worker and he's a lawyer. They're invited to *Seders* and feel very comfortable. He tells his colleagues that his sister is Jewish and sends me *Hanukkah* cards.

Mom gave me all these things and told me to always love Judaism. I distinctly remember her saying, "Always honor it; always protect it." She never said be Jewish. She said we were Jews in Spain, and it was always important to us. Mom said, "Don't ever let anyone around you disrespect it."

At this point I felt honored. These things are so beautiful. I knew I'd treasure them my whole life. I never saw it as a conflict at this point. It was a relief that she told me because everything seemed to make more sense. I didn't know that my siblings had not known that I had been told this. My sister who doesn't practice anything, but considers herself Catholic, still doesn't want to know anything about our past.

I went to Catholic high school. Actually, all of us went to Catholic schools at one point or another, I might add, although only my oldest brother, Bob, and I went all twelve years, plus kindergarten, to Catholic schools. I did have some more battles in high school. Anti-proselytizing of anything was strong in my family. I would argue doctrine. In the Catholic Church, doctrine is doctrine and you don't give an opinion. It's not *Talmudic*, not logical. I wanted things to make sense. When I asked them to explain things, I was told it's a sin if you doubt anything. You couldn't ask questions or give opinions. I had trouble with doctrine but had no trouble with school or people. I wasn't hostile to the Catholic Church. I loved the music in the church and the ritual and the literature, etc.

Mimi knew the Old Testament very well. Mimi explained scriptures to my mother all the time (she died before I was born). After I studied the *Talmud*, I realized that Mimi had already told *Talmudic* things to my mother. Mom gave me the *Talmud* during my high school years. Through these stories Mimi told my mother—and then my mother would pass them on to me—I realized that Mimi was very knowledgeable about the *Talmud*.

Apparently, it was stated, the family left Spain, Aragon, and went to Santo Domingo. It was never said that they were hiding. I don't know if they were *conversos*. Once they got to Santo Domingo, I don't know what happened to that group. Others went to Morocco and practiced Judaism there. Then they went to Mexico where they had to hide and apparently become crypto-Jews. My Great-Grandmother Mimi was born in Hermosillo, a desert-like area in northwest Mexico, near California.

I didn't know my mother's family spoke Ladino. I thought it was a bizarre type of Spanish, a strange dialect, until I heard and learned Ladino. My mother was open about *Sabbath* (Saturday) blessings. She would sometimes light candles Friday night, but not always on Friday night. Often, she lit votive candles to saints. She had great and genuine devotion to various saints. I thought, was she really concealing it, or was it done that way in her family? She always said blessings on me with her hands on my head when I left to go somewhere. "May you always be like Rachel and Esther." I saw *Fiddler on the Roof* and saw the same thing. I thought that could be Catholic. She took holy water and made the sign of the cross on my forehead. She said a Jewish prayer, a *Shabbat* prayer: "May His face shine upon you; May He give you peace."

I remember when I was little and we moved into a new house. Mom and I were walking and went up on a porch of an empty house that was for sale, just to look. Mom was all excited when she saw a *mezuzah*. I was told every Jewish home has a *mezuzah*. "You have to kiss it when you go in. It is a blessing and protects Jewish houses, and it's a sign that Jewish people live there." We didn't have one. We had holy water in a small tiny basin near the right doorpost. We kissed it when we went in and out. I was wondering if that was Catholic, but I have enough Catholic background to know that many Catholic families didn't do it.

My mother's family legitimately has a history of migraines. I was reading Inquisition documents where people were turned in because a servant would say, "My mistress has a migraine every Friday night to Saturday night." You couldn't get out of bed and couldn't do anything, so you claimed to have a migraine.

We did eat pork, but my mother DID teach me to kosher chickens and never deal with animal blood, at a young age. Now I'm a vegetarian, and I keep kosher.

I came fully back to Judaism about six years ago. I was split for so long, thinking I'm supposed to be Catholic because I was raised Catholic. As I read more Jewish books, I felt someone was explaining how I thought. I was hearing my thoughts and belief system on paper. I realized that I'm so naturally Jewish. This is how I am! I made a decision to go and be happy and comfortable, rather than constantly fight to be Catholic out of loyalty. But, I realized I wasn't naturally that way; so why torture yourself. (Square peg in round hole syndrome!) I think about how families react. My brother Bob, my oldest brother, said my mother never told him anything, but he believes me. He's the only one who believes this actually happened. It wasn't like my mother was hiding anything; I just had a different and closer relationship with both of my parents than any of my older siblings. The reason is my father retired from the CIA and moved here to El Paso. I lived here from the time I was eighteen. My brothers and sisters lived a different life. They never moved here and never had any experience in the Southwest and with Spanish culture. They had a totally different life on the East Coast than I did.

They didn't know that part of my mother. My parents were here. By this time I was an adult. That's when I really got to know my parents, where the rest of the family didn't have the opportunity. My sister didn't want to know because she felt Irish all the time and didn't want to be confused.

With the name Greene, people always thought I was Jewish. I look the most different than the rest of my family. I'm the only one with very dark hair, and with totally different features—eyes, mouth, etc. My sister does have dark brown hair, but it has more red in it. Her eyes are lighter brown, and she has lots of freckles—so looks quite Irish. My mother would brush my hair when I was little and say, "You're the one that looks like the de Lunas."

**Molly Longoria and Woodrow E. Longoria (Mother and son)**

### Molly

My name was actually Amalia Sánchez, my maiden name and a Jewish name. We discovered that this was a Jewish name in the last thirteen years. Other names in the family were Lucero, Montoya (both sides of the family), and Torrez, on Mother's side. This group that came up together from Monterrey, Mexico, went to Canon Blanco, near Albuquerque. My great-grandparents went to the Bernalillo area, which was called Canon Blanco. This place to where the Jews came was like a refugee camp. From there, they dispersed to areas of northern New Mexico and southern Colorado. These were all mountain areas. My understanding was that, in order to recognize the group when they dispersed, they changed all the names with s's to z's. Everyone around here has z's instead of s's in their names. A group in the Monterrey area told us this. They are in a real isolated area in Monterrey, not in the city itself. Some people I know, missionaries, went down there. They were the ones that had told us about this whole little village, outside of Monterrey, that knew they were Jews. They didn't hide it.

Father's side settled in the Rociada area, northwest of Las Vegas. Mother's side went to the Conejos area in southern Colorado. We finally settled in the Rociada area until World War II. People in the family had biblical names such as Moisés, Saloman, Seferino (Sephardic), Ruben, Benjamin, and Gabriel. We also had Hebrew names found in the scriptures.

It was continually pounded into us that we were Spanish, from Spain, and that we had no connection to Mexico. My dad and mother did this. All of my grandparents did this. My mother's grandfather would always say, "Never forget that we came from Spain." Father continued this, and he would say it to the grandchildren. I tried to talk to my aunts and they always told the children, as they would be walking out in the field, "Remember, we are Spanish." My grandfather prayed continually, but I don't remember the prayers. Dad's father prayed all day long. He, the Sánchez grandfather, avoided, which was probably a Jewish thing, the Penitentes. He would have nothing to do with them. My other grandfather, on my mother's side, was a Penitente. I have one of his little books. The prayers were so strange and didn't resemble Catholicism. The majority of the people around here were Penitentes. There were *morada*s in every little village. It was a secret society. Even women were not permitted in it. The men were real secretive. They would eat and pray in the *morada*s. They would stay at night and pray. They slept and ate there. They didn't work. Then they would leave and go up into the mountains and do sacrificial things. They also wore white outfits. I don't know why they wore them. They would sacrifice themselves, flagellation. A lot of it was on their knees, crawling on their knees, up in the mountains, in hiding.

My family never told us anything. I think they knew and didn't want to talk about it. The older people in the mountains, where I grew up, didn't admit anything. Secretiveness was in certain areas. Part of the family became Presbyterians. My grandfather immediately joined the Presbyterian Church before the 1950s. They joined so that they could read the Old Testament. We were not permitted Bibles in this area of northern New Mexico until about the fifties. My family held out. Great-Grandmother taught Dad scripture from the Old Testament. Dad died in the eighties, and up until that time, still remembered scriptures his grandmother taught him. There were discoveries of homemade headstones with Stars of David on them. Up until the sixties, there were chapels in the Catholic Church in New Mexico. They just had a visiting priest. Men sat in the back and women sat in the front.

One of the reasons I don't remember that I was Jewish is because there was never any indication. As a child, I grew up in the mountains of Colorado. My father would bring us down three or four times a year if something was going on. We came through Las Vegas and went to the farm. One year, my grandmother brought me to Las Vegas, and we went grocery shopping. On her side were the Rudolphs, Ashkenazim, and they were Jewish people. I remember, and I've never forgotten. We were walking on the sidewalk and going to one of the stores. We saw an orthodox man, and my grandmother said we have to cross the street because one of those who killed Christ was walking there. Yet, her family was Ashkenazi. Her father was Lucero. The Rudolphs were on her mother's side. I never even knew there was anything such as a Jewish person. We were close to the Rudolphs, but nobody ever said they were Jews. The Rudolphs married into the Lucero and Martínez families. My grandmother was a product of the *converso* and Ashkenazi heritage. Perhaps, she thought she would feel repercussions from neighbors. People who admit they're Jews don't have a real connection to the rest of the people.

You did not find intermarriages with other nationalities. I found it strange that in our families we were not to marry outside our own people. A first cousin to my father married outside. It was hush-hush, and it was a shame. Eventually, when the young man went east, where he was from, she stayed here. With us, it was laid out black and white. You marry within your own heritage. We had never been exposed to white people from Mexico and other territories. Yet, they married into the Jews of Ashkenazi descent. That was allowed. They probably knew it was part of their heritage. Both sides of the family had Ashkenazi heritage. Our Spanish language was different.

When I married my husband, there was a lot of opposition. Yet, it was an arranged marriage. In our family, girls were married by the time they were fourteen because they were frightened of girls becoming pregnant. My husband came up and asked for my hand in marriage. This wasn't a typically arranged marriage. My father agreed and my husband had to agree to certain rules. I was immediately taken out of school. That was the last marriage that was arranged. I was never asked. My father or mother never asked if I wanted to marry this man.

All members of the family married relatives. Sometimes, they didn't know that they were such close relatives. Kids didn't realize this, and it wasn't discussed. One thing that did happen was that you went to church and had the ceremony. Following the ceremony, you went home. Musicians followed the bride and groom, and the rest of the party followed. It was like a parade. This was in Frederic, Colorado. They marched us five blocks to my aunt's house. Coming home from church, you saw the wine and glasses on a round table. There was lots of food to eat. Traditionally, the celebration continued into the next day. The bride and groom couldn't leave until the whole thing broke up. This is still a custom today.

We didn't have Christmas trees and most people didn't exchange gifts. They would give a coin, like a nickel, to the children. Most of the people here did not do that. I don't know if it had anything to do with the Ashkenazim. We ate *empanadas* during Christmas. They were mostly made of dried fruit. We ate special foods during Lent. We ate *panocha*, made from sprouted wheat. This was the unleavened bread. During Lent, everything was baked way ahead of time. Grandfather, on my mother's side, was a Penitente. He wore white pajama-type clothing during Lent, but I don't know what it signified. He must have worn it in the *morada*s.

I came out of the Catholic Church to the Presbyterian Church. I heard an Ashkenazi teacher, Burt Yellen, speak. I had never heard teaching with so much wisdom and knowledge. It was such an experience that I cried the whole time. I felt that I was home, but I didn't know why. It wasn't until I started dragging my family to the Messianic Synagogue, and he came up to us one day and said, "You are Jewish." This was in 1987. He was sitting there, and said, "Look at that face. You cannot deny this. You have to look into it." Some of my nieces and nephews look Jewish.

At that point, we came away kind of stunned. What is this guy saying here? That's when we started looking into it. I couldn't approach my dad. We started researching it, reading about the Sephardic Jews, the history behind it. We thought of the history of our families, coming up through Monterrey, and how they were so emphatic about us being Spanish, from Spain, and not being anything else. We came up in the 1600s. That's as far back as we know about in this area.

We made *biscochitos*. I have so many Jewish books and Jewish cookbooks that had the cookies in there. These cookies were cut in the same shapes as my grandmother's cookies. Everyone in the area did this. It looked like a pinwheel. I don't think it was Ashkenazi.

We had holy water in special containers nailed to the door and touched it when we went out. We used special knives to kill chickens. The cows were strung up from the hind feet and the vein would be cut. Blood was allowed to drain. I thought the meat was salted for preserving it. My grandparents did not avoid blood. They would use the blood for cooking on my dad's side, but not on my mother's side. Eggs with blood spots were not eaten and thrown out. Eight days after the baby was born, a prayer was said. I thought this was a Catholic thing. The name came with the baptism.

There was a twenty-four hour burial. I thought it was because they had no choice. When someone died, he was laid out at home, washed and cleaned. Then they would have an all-night vigil. People would stay with the deceased. Coins were placed on the eyes of the deceased. The whole village would come, and the burial was the next day. People did bring food after the burial. I do remember that people would come and sit with the family. It went on for a few days. There was a one-year mourning period.

My dad would talk about this all the time. In my grandfather's generation, there weren't any coffins. They would dig a grave six feet down and carve out a cave. Then, they would wrap the body in a white sheet and place it in the grave. I've seen stones placed on headstones. This is still done. Both sides had Ashkenazi influence. In the fifties, there were stones used as markers rather than headstones. We've always seen pebbles on them. The family was not aware of their Sephardic heritage. Mirrors were covered or turned when someone died. Grandfather made bonfires on top of the mountain. Then the neighbors across the mountains would light bonfires. When I asked my father about this, he became very quiet. The Ashkenazim came about 1835. My father told me about the bonfires when he was a young man. Kosher wine was always there. Great-Grandmother was a Rudolf, an Ashkenazi. She married a Lucero who was from Spain, my grandmother's father.

On Mother's side of the family, my mother's grandmother was an Ashkenazi. Her name was Green. She married a Torrez. We never celebrated Easter the way it was celebrated. We would go to the church service, but we didn't do the Easter thing. The Catholic Church was all we had.

A synagogue was built, before the fifties, in Las Vegas, the first one in the state of New Mexico. I was never aware of it. By this time, my grandparents wouldn't have gone to synagogue. They felt it would be a great shame to leave the Catholic Church. This feeling still exists today. When I, one sister, and a sister-in-law left the Catholic Church, in Colorado, Dad came crying, "To go back home now, I will be going home like a donkey with my ears hanging down." It was a shame to lift his head coming to New Mexico. We never associated ourselves with Mexico, other than coming through it.

Why did I leave the Catholic Church? In the seventies, I was active in the Catholic Church. The group I was with had a new priest. Everyone decided they wanted Bible study. He said he would have it in homes because it would be questioned in church. He claimed, "I would love to learn the Bible. We were never taught about the Bible." And he was in the seminary for seven years. In Colorado, ten of us studied the Old Testament. We had the Bible studies in our homes.

What I had been taught growing up was not in the New Testament scriptures. It didn't line up. After the Catholic Church, I went to a non-denominational church. We read the New and Old Testaments. It was a Born Again Church. They didn't have specific doctrine. We just studied the Old and

New Testaments. I found that what we had been taught growing up bore a resemblance to the Old Testament.

We stayed in Colorado for a long time. We raised our family there and came back to the mountains of Las Vegas in 1980. My grandparents, from my mother's side, were there. It's amazing that there's any residue left, that we would know who we were even though we had been dispersed.

### Woodrow Eugene Longoria

I feel a strong connection to Judaism. My grandfather and uncles were violinists. I'm very comfortable with Judaism. My brother embraced it. I grew up Catholic. It didn't feel right to me. It was not the truth. Something was missing. It's my soul that's connected to Judaism.

### Orfa Salinas

Governor Carvajal was governor of Nuevo Leon. The area of Nuevo Leon went from Tampico, Mexico, up to San Antonio,

Texas, near Veracruz, and then across. South Texas was part of that area of Nuevo Leon, part of New Spain.

The Inquisition was established in Mexico, but it wasn't very active at this time. People were practicing Judaism, and they became a little too careless, too open. They were becoming an embarrassment. The Inquisition then became more active, and they even imprisoned Governor Carvajal and his nephew who had the same name. His nephew was very outspoken about it, and the whole immediate family eventually died at the hands of the Inquisition.

The second in command to Carvajal might be one of my ancestors. His last name was Sosa. I don't know, but I suspect it. I'm working on this research.

The original Carvajal was imprisoned. They let him go. They came back and imprisoned him again. They took him back to Mexico City. All the cities that he established are in northeastern Mexico, and all my ancestors came from that area. I've traced them back to the late 1600s. Names traced were Franco, which was my mother's last name, Torres, Salinas, Sosa, and González. The above is both sides of the family. Mom's side is more suspicious because her parents are first cousins. First cousins married first cousins all the time. I feel there's more of a connection to the Sephardic heritage, if at all, on Mom's side. I didn't know my dad's family as well.

Governor Carvajal was imprisoned the second time. Before he did that, he put this man, the second in command, in charge of taking care of the people. When Sosa realized that Carvajal was not going to be coming back, he gathered up as many of the families as he could in a group and decided to escape before they'd come and get the rest of them. The official story in most of the history books is that Sosa was arrogant and decided to go and explore New Mexico without permission from the Spanish government.

This is the other theory: He gathered the people together and brought them up to New Mexico to escape. All the families with these names came to New Mexico. It was the first time any Spaniards had come up to New Mexico. When the people from the Inquisition realized that they had come up here, as far as Española, they sent soldiers to get them. They were brought back to Mexico City. I don't believe all of them came up here in the first place. I think some of them stayed up here and didn't go back to Mexico City. They could have hidden in the mountains. They got away before they came and got them. It would have been easy for them to wander off on their own before these people from Mexico City came for them. I think before they got to Mexico City some of them might have escaped also.

I was never told I had a Jewish heritage. When I spoke to my mother the first time about it, I don't know if she called my aunt or my aunt called her. My mother came from another room and said she had to go to my aunt's house. She told me to drive her. When I got there, we sat around the table. I had no idea why we went there. My cousin was there. They already knew about the conversation I had had at home with my siblings. I don't remember the exact details. All of a sudden I found myself being ambushed by these three people. My aunt said, "So what if you're Jewish." My cousin was the most hostile. She said things like, "So now you think you're better than everybody else because you found out we're Jewish." She said, "I know we're Jewish. I worked on our genealogy and found out we were Jewish. So what! It doesn't make any difference." Basically what they were telling me was that they wanted me to stop talking about it. This was about five or six years ago.

What had first started me off researching this was when I ran across an article about *Hanukkah*. It mentioned *Hanukkah* foods that I had had all my childhood. We'd always have them around Christmas. They were *buñuelos*. That stayed on the back of my mind, and I didn't think about it much. Later on, I ran across another article, and this one was from

*La Herencia.* And that one was about crypto-Jews. I started reading. The article had a list of words that are Ladino, not Spanish, which were used in my family. It had a list of names from the Inquisition trials. Every single one of my family's last names was there on that list. Dad's grandmother was Ramírez. That was listed. I have Ramírez on both sides. On Mother's side I have a great-grandmother who was Gómez. That's what started me researching crypto-Jews and working on my genealogy.

It wasn't so much the rituals, but the way of thinking. They were secretive. The people we associated with were a close-knit group of family—related people and some friends. We were not the same as other Hispanics because we had no crosses in the house. Some people have little worship centers. We never had that. There were no pictures of saints—no idols. We never worshiped with crosses or saints. We never wore crosses around our necks. On my dad's side we were Catholics, who never went to church. We were Catholic in name only. On my mother's side they are Baptists. They are very, very strict about kneeling. They hated the Catholic Church and called them idol worshipers. We are also not like other Hispanics because of the food we ate. I grew up eating *tacos* that don't have cheese on them.

When Mother killed chickens she did it by cutting the neck and hanging them so that the blood could run out. She slit the neck quickly. We didn't eat blood. Some people eat blood sausages, but we didn't. We would cut off the nerve or something, part of the chicken. My mother always broke the eggs in a bowl before she made them into scrambled eggs. If an egg had blood spots, she threw it out. Mom said that the egg was no good because it had a baby on it. You can't eat it when you see a little piece of an embryo on the egg yolk. I grew up thinking that's disgusting. You can't eat a baby. Occasionally, at a wedding, they might kill a goat, and a goat was killed the same way, hung by its hind legs to drain the blood.

My grandfather, when he prayed, spoke of there being one God. He is the most powerful. He had a prayer book that had Hebrew on one side and Spanish on the other. I like this prayer book because it feels very familiar. In this Baptist Church, most of these people were my relatives or close friends. We had traditions similar to Jewish traditions. For instance, on New Year's Eve (U.S. New Year's Eve) we would go to the Baptist Church and spend all evening praying. After midnight, the prayers would end. Afterwards we would go into the fellowship hall where everybody would share a huge potluck meal together. I think it's similar to what people do on *Yom Kippur*. Most people in the United States, on New Year's Eve, party or have fireworks. We would go to church and pray. I consider myself Jewish. In my family and in the extended family, it's a given that you go to college. It's expected.

We didn't have a *bar mitzvah*, but from the time I was nine years old till thirteen, we had to go to school, after regular school, at the church to learn how to read and write Spanish. We learned Spanish by reading the Spanish Bible. We studied the Old and New Testament. Both boys and girls did this. When I turned thirteen, we went in front of the church, and the minister asked us questions. And we were baptized. Then we were considered grownups.

Grandfather, my mother's dad, was one of the elders in the community. People used to come to visit him and ask advice. He didn't drive and walked everywhere. He would walk to people's houses if he knew someone was sick. He would pray with them. He was one of the older members of the community so he was respected. He knew a lot about the Bible, and he always spoke in terms of giving you advice by some story in the Bible. He always talked about God. Religion has always been very important in my family. The thinking was that God was part of life. It's like spirituality as compared to religion. My Baptist Church prayed to Jesús. My extended family believes that there's only one God. On the other hand, they also constantly emphasize the Trinity (God, the Son, and the Holy Ghost). This is how they explained that they're not breaking God's commandment to worship only one God. Jesús is the son of God. The Trinity says that God and the Son of God, Jesús, are the same.

I found out later about some of the foods that we ate. We ate corn *tortillas* for Passover because flour *tortillas* had leavening and baking powder. We ate scrambled eggs with *nopalito* (cactus). That was a dish eaten as a meal. We ate cilantro (green-like parsley). I don't remember when these things were eaten. Other people who did more research than I said these were Passover foods. We didn't observe Lent. I was raised in South Texas and came to New Mexico about nine years ago. I was raised thinking that everything that happens is because God makes it happen. I don't like New Mexico, and I've been wanting to leave since I got here. I think that if I never had gotten here, I would never have discovered all these things. We would sweep towards the center of the room because of not wanting dust on the *mezuzah*. This was found out recently. We were told to "Keep the *Sabbath* holy." They considered the *Sabbath* as being Sunday. We worshiped and read the Bible at home. A special meal was prepared. We didn't work on Sunday, as it was a day of rest.

I don't think anybody in their right mind would want to be Jewish if they weren't. Once you're known as possibly being Jewish, there might be another Hitler. Some people assume that you don't have very good self esteem about who you are, about being a Hispanic, and think you want to be Jewish because you want to be better than what you really are. I have a cousin who works as a scientist at NASA. I was a food microbiologist. My daughter is in her second year of Harvard Law School. There is no reason for us to feel inferior. This is the best time, as far as being fearful in America, to speak about it because Jews right now have it the best they ever had it. I feel that I can't afford not to do it now. I think that God wanted me to find out who I really was. The Sephardics are dying out. He wants us to come back to the Jewish religion.

What made me join a synagogue? It's like a mission.

We're supposed to go back to Judaism. My generation was close-knit and married within their own. I've lived all over the United States and met so many other people, and now is when people are intermarrying others. The Civil Rights Movement changed that. Now the children are going out into the world. If we don't find out now that we're Jewish, before long it will be lost.

When my grandmother, Dad's mother, was to be buried, we had her in the house. Women were inside and the men were outside of the house. I had to go and kiss her. The men and women were separate. The women were crying and the men were having conversations. The first thing was to cover the mirrors. The women wore black.

My daughter was lactose intolerant. She outgrew it. Father had psoriasis. I read that this was a Jewish thing. Father's family came to New Spain from France, but they're Spanish. My mother makes food with Turkish tendencies. We ate eggplant, figs, and certain spices for cooking. How many Hispanics do you know who like eggplant? We were very superstitious. Mom said, "If you drop something on the ground, you have to kiss it." When we were learning how to drive, my sister backed out of the driveway too quickly. Mom said, "Be careful; you might kill a Christian."

Orfa is a Ladino name. It's the Spanish version of a Hebrew name, Ofra. I'm named after Orfa Linda Castro. A few cousins have the same name. Some names in the family are Samuel and Benito, which means blessed in Spanish. My sister is Dalia, a common name in Israel. My name is common in Israel. Rabin's daughter is Dalia, a member of the Knesset. There's a Moisés in the family in Grandfather's generation.

## Richard Chávez

## Author

I met Richard Chávez in San Felipe de Neri Church in Albuquerque. Richard directed my attention to the Star of David on the top right and top left of the altar. He was acting as a guide by answering visitors' questions. Also mentioned was that the church was two hundred years old and had a crypto-Jewish heritage.

## Richard

My father's side came from Spain. The names on my mother's side include García. They are also from Spain. "An aunt on Dad's side told me that I had a Jewish heritage. My aunt went to school in Santa Fe and had a good education. She practiced Judaism in secret. She lit candles on Friday night and also lit *Hanukkah* candles. She told me everything. She told me of Passover. When my aunt prayed, she didn't want anyone to bother her. She prayed inside, and went into a room to pray away from people. However, people knew about it.

My parents took me to church, and my aunt took me to a temple on Fourth Street when I was young. My mother's side didn't talk about their heritage. It was known to me that my great-grandparents were Jewish.

## Author

The family believed in circumcision. They also drained the blood of animals. I asked Richard if most people who attended this church had a Sephardic heritage, and his answer was, "Yes."

## Richard Valdéz

I always knew about my Judaism. I was afraid of what they'd say and thought they wouldn't understand me. A cousin did genealogy study at Highlands University. She uncovered information that Mom's family came from Andalusia. Both

Mom's and Dad's family came to New Spain in the 1600s. I think they're cousins.

Mom's name, Luján, in the old Ladino language meant luxury. Dad's name, Valdéz, meant valley in Spain. They're both Sephardic names.

Some of the family came with Don Diego de Vargas. A cousin said that when the family left Spain they were *Judíos* (Jews). They were *conversos* during the Inquisition. The family was called *Marranos* because they didn't observe kosher laws. The cousin said that Christianity was brought upon them, that they had to convert. They were forced. They later became devout Christians.

One of my grandfathers was a prayer leader (*hermano*) in the Penitentes. The main apostolic ministry of the Brotherhood of Penitentes was the corporate works of mercy, caring for the sick, visiting the sick, helping widows, and community things for the Brotherhood such as burial.

At one time in New Mexico, the clergy disappeared so the Brotherhood acted as the ministry for what the clergy normally did. I believe the Penitentes were crypto-Jews. In the *morada*s they have a *menorah*, a southwestern *menorah*. Penitentes pray in Ladino. They say *kaddish*, improvised from what Jews do. They light candles for the dead during services—Novenas for nine days. They believe that their souls will be delivered from the elements of purgatory. This organization came from Spain in Sevilla. They make noise called *maracas*. I believe it originates from Judaism. They use chains, hammers, or anything to make noise. For every Hispanic man who belongs to a *morada*, the oldest son is initiated into the society so the society won't die out.

Growing up in Cheyenne, Wyoming, I was raised by Mom's parents who were devout Roman Catholics. Both grandparents were from northern New Mexico. The most striking thing that hit me was that every time my grandmother would leave the house, she would kiss the door of the house. She would make a cross as a disguise. She kissed the door to protect the household. When asked why she did it, she said her mother and grandmother did it. She would say something from the Old Testament. It was Christianized.

I've always felt connected to Judaism. A custom that I grew up with was that Mom's mother always prayed and lit candles on Fridays to her Christian statues. One candle was by itself for the Holy Souls. It was not near any Christian images. I think it symbolized Judaism. It amazed me that she would cup her hand outward, and in a kneeling position, she would pray when she lit candles. I think that also symbolized Judaism.

The thing that really stuck in my mind was that my grandmother never swept the floor until Saturday evening when the sun went down because Christ was resting. This was a Jewish thing that was Christianized. I always knew in my heart that we were different. I grew up as a devout Roman Catholic. The community where I lived was Irish Catholic, and their customs were different than those in the Hispanic community.

The original *Sabbath* was when the sun went down on Friday. *Sabbath* means *Sábado*. *Sábado* means the *Sabbath*. A priest friend said an early pope changed the *Sabbath* to Sunday. All of my great aunts lit candles on Friday and called Sunday the *Sabbath.*

Another New Mexico custom of Hispanic Catholics is the celebration of the Feast of St. Esther in the Catholic Church. The people were afraid of anti-Semitism. Esther is the queen who delivered the Jews. On her day, in New Mexico, the Spanish people would bake *empanaditas* filled with meat or fruit. Mom's mother was a big influence in my life. She would cook fruit such as prunes and pumpkin, place it on the dough, and press down the sides with her finger.

Another custom is that every time we would leave to visit a relative, we would kneel and receive a blessing from our grandparents.  Grandmother and Grandfather would touch us on the head and make a cross on our foreheads.  I try to revive some family customs.  I have a *mezuzah*.

When my cousin in Wyoming killed sheep, he was careful with the blood.  They drained the blood.  When they drained the blood, they covered it up with the earth.  When they killed a sheep, they didn't drink milk when eating the meat.

My grandmother, every time there was thunder or the clouds were black, would go outside and throw salt. Grandmother threw salt up into the sky. Another custom, when the babies were young, was to put water on their heads. I was convinced of my Jewish heritage because my other friends didn't do this in Cheyenne, Wyoming.  Our family was from northern New Mexico.

A Jewish woman in Cheyenne said that our family was very Jewish and we were in denial.  The Catholic Church is different here because of the Spanish influence.  It's more emotional here.  People are more devout here.  It's also different because of the Jewish influence.  When I told a priest in Wyoming about our Jewish heritage, he said, "Hogwash!"

A priest in town said that a woman prays in Ladino during confession.  My grandmother would pray some stuff in Ladino. I think that if all Sephardic people would come to realize their heritage, there would be a revival. I'm a monk and church is natural to me.  In the synagogue, I don't understand Hebrew. I haven't found a place where I feel comfortable.

The chants in the *morada* are from the Old Testament. We sing *The Song of Songs*.  I want this brought out.

I couldn't wait to meet you because it was like something coming out of my body to find my true identity.

**Robert J. Ortega**

During my youth, I grew up oblivious to Judaism. I attended Catholic schools and church and never looked past my own little world. In college, I was first exposed to Judaism and realized what it was, and gained some knowledge. In looking back at my early years, I remember things that the women did which may be Jewish rituals.

My grandmother and her lady friends and relatives were very inquisitive when introduced to a new friend. They would ask what family they were from and would either say nothing, or "they are good people."

I also remember when people died. People generally didn't do much until after the eight-day mass. Then you were expected to behave like you did during Lent (no dances, no movies, etc.) for a year. I remember that if someone was widowed at a young age, that person was frowned on if it looked like they were getting on with life before the year was up.

I remember that virtually all of my friends and relatives had biblical names. I have a niece named Dawn, born in 1970, and we could never have my elderly grandmother understand that her name was Dawn, not Donna or a derivative of Don. Also, in my younger days, it was very rare for a man to have kitchen skills. My grandmother always did the cooking. In visiting relatives, you would almost always be in the kitchen and the matriarchal woman would be cooking and feeding guests as they visited.

I definitely feel some connection being a businessman. I grew up and wondered where the work ethic came from for the successful businessmen in an area where not everyone was successful. In my observations in my mature life, I see many parallels to the Jewish merchants in major cities and the successful merchants in the small Spanish communities. I can't say I have a real spiritual tie, but wonder why movies like *Fiddler on the Roof* and *Yentl* are among my favorites. I have a definite curiosity and feel this is the result of ties to Judaism.

**Author**

During my visit to the Ortega Weaving Shop (the family business), I asked Robert if I could speak to his father. The answer was, "Yes," and I met with this very elegant and dignified elderly gentlemen. My questioning lasted for about fifteen minutes, trying various approaches. He always answered that he didn't know anything. At the end of the conversation, he finally said, "You'll never get anything out of me."

**Rodolfo Proenza**

I always felt that there was something special about my family. I knew our last name was unique, but wasn't sure as to why I felt different. My father told me to always honor the Jewish people and to bless them. It wasn't until I was thirty-three years old that my uncle told me that we had a Jewish heritage. My aunt (his sister) confirmed this as well.

I've heard that my grandfather would not step into a church and disliked icons. I believe mirrors were turned over after a death in the family, but it is not something that the family practices today. As far as kosher practices, we avoided eggs with blood spots. My mother mourned the passing of my father for a year by wearing dark clothing.

As far as my connection to Judaism, I feel that I lost thirty-three years of my life by not knowing of my heritage. When I go to temple services, I love the prayers, reading of *Torah*, and wearing a *kippah*. I desire to embrace more of Judaism as I become aware of it. I want to be part of the Jewish community. I want the blessings of the God of Israel! The

Proenza family migrated from Portugal to the Azore Islands. It is possible that they went to North Africa before settling in the Caribbean (Cuba). The family surnames that might have Jewish ties are Proenza (Proencas in Portuguese), Portelles, Rodríguez, Vega, and Hernández.

### Ruth Rael

Dad's name was Matías Archuleta. Mom's name was Lucía García.

My parents were born and raised in Saguache, Colorado. The family, on both sides, lived there. Basically, we were all related in Saguache. We also married within the group.

Burial was within twenty-four hours. When I was growing up, we covered mirrors when someone died. We mourned for about a year a long time ago. This is not done now. When a person died, we would put a quarter on the eyes of the deceased to close his eyes. On the one-year anniversary of a person's death, my grandparents lit a candle for the deceased in the house. This is not done now. They also said Mass on the year anniversary, at least for the first year. They would throw a handful of dirt in the grave at the time of the burial.

We had chickens at home. If we saw blood in the yolk of the egg, we would feed it to the dogs. We avoided blood. I would cringe at the mere mention of blood. When animals were killed, they were hung to drain the blood. When females went into the church, they covered their heads. When I was growing up, the men had to wear jackets.

Advent time was the period beginning four Sundays before Christmas. Before Christmas, a candle is lit to prepare for Christmas. Most of the names, a long time ago, were biblical names from the Old Testament, such as Matías. We have Aaron in the family—my husband and son. My name is Ruth.

*Panocha*s were eaten during Lent as the unleavened bread. First, I cleaned and washed the wheat. The wheat was then spread on the table to dry and sprout. After it sprouted, we ground the wheat and made it into flour. The roots of the wheat were also used. No yeast was added. However, we added whole-wheat flour and brown sugar to about two cups of *panocha* flour. Boiling the mixture was next. This was the method of making *panocha*s. It tends to be like a pudding.

After the birth of a child, women stayed in the house for a long period of time. I didn't do this. I don't know if I have this heritage. I don't feel a connection to Judaism. I never asked my family about this heritage. We were far removed from everything. I'm getting all curious about this Jewish heritage.

**Teodoro Rael**

Family names included García, Fernández, Santistevan, and Valdéz. Anaya is a surname on my maternal side. Her maiden name was Vigil. Vigil is the name of a town in northern Spain. (Jews who left Spain after the expulsion often took the names of the towns from where they came.) On my paternal side, my father's mother's name was Prandi-Valdéz. Grandma was Prandi because of her father and Valdéz because of her mother. She was born in Valdéz, New Mexico, but the Prandi side of the family came from Llano de Alba, Italy. My ancestor, Carlo Prandi, was born in 1836 and came here when he was fifteen years old. Rael was on my father's side, my grandfather's name.

No one ever told us we were Jewish. In fact, the family denies that we were Jews. We had a reunion about five years ago where the connection to Judaism was denied. I've been to Spain. In Granada, it was said that the name Rael is not Jewish. It is Arabic. Father Martínez Díaz, in Lorca, Spain, is doing some research for me. The mayor of Santa Fe, Granada, said the name is not Jewish. Father Díaz, a military chaplain who came from Lorca, said there is a possibility that the spelling was Rayel. We are of the same line as the Rael family in Questa. I lived south of Questa, in Hondo.

The men on my father's side and my mother's side avoided church. We speak an archaic Spanish, Ladino. Spanish exchange students told the father of the girl who I was housing that we speak old, archaic Spanish. I participated with Grandma Anaya (maternal side) in the Penitentes house of worship. The women wore shawls over their heads. The Prandi side didn't believe in the Penitentes. The men avoided it. However, even if you weren't a member of the Penitentes, the people participated in their processions on Good Friday.

Priests said you should only name children after Catholic saints. The Church would not baptize the child if he were not given a saint's name. My mom's name is Ester. My great-grandfather's name was Moisés, although he was on the Italian side of the family. I have a cousin, my father's sister's son, named Moisés. He was probably named after the great-grandfather.

We would butcher the animals on the ranch by cutting their throats and then hanging them to drain the blood. We ate the blood. We ate everything—heart, kidney, etc. When someone died, we would have a wake for two or three days. After the burial, we would stay in the house and people visited. There was an eight-day mass after the death, including the days of the wake. There was a one-year anniversary mass every year after the person's death. This is still done.

During a wedding ceremony, the hands of the bride and groom were bound with a rosary, the *Laco* ritual. Those who chose to follow the tradition only did this. At this time, a prayer was said. *Panocha* was eaten during Lent. All families did this. I remember that we lit bonfires Christmas Eve. The bonfires symbolized lighting the way for the coming of the infant Jesús. Mom would sweep away from the door. The

Raels came from Lorca. Father Martínez Díaz said the Rael name came from *Morato*. That was a derogatory term.

I think we might have a connection to Judaism, but I'm still curious and still searching. Research is continuing within the family.

**Tessie Rael Ortega**

Aaron Rael is my first cousin. Our dads were brothers. My dad was José Praxedes. Grandfather was Eliseo Rael. Grandmother was Inocensia Gómez de Rael. On Mom's side, Grandmother was Salome Valdéz and Grandfather was Roberto Gallegos. Mom's name was Esther Gallegos.

We were told that we were Jewish by a first cousin, Alex Rael, who went to New York City. He found Raels in the telephone book. He contacted them and was told that Raels are Jewish.

We would light candles on the year anniversary of a loved-one's death. When I was small, I heard that you light candles for people who are dead. My grandmother covered the mirrors when someone died, and relatives stayed around for about a week after burial. People brought food to the home of the deceased, and the family observed one year of mourning. The men didn't shave for a month after the death of a relative. I was told to keep customs secret, and I couldn't tell anyone. After slaughtering an animal, the family hung the animal downward so that the blood would drain, a practice still continued today. The meat was then soaked and salted. Eggs with blood spots were disposed of, thus avoiding blood.

Passover (Easter) was considered Holy Week (*Semana Santa*). The family cleaned the house and used different dishes, a custom taught by my mother. *Tortillas* and biscuits were the unleavened bread eaten during Passover, and they did not rise because yeast was not used. Wood was chopped before Passover, and we couldn't work all week. Radio or music was not permitted. My first cousin told me to keep the *Sabbath* (Saturday) holy. We would play a game called *pon y quita da—pon,* meaning put; *quita*, meaning take; *da*, meaning give. *Empanadas* were eaten during Christmas

We were told that we didn't pronounce words correctly. We were called *Mochos* because we cut words short.

Alonso Rael de Aguilar, my ancestor, came, according to the family, because he was persecuted in Spain. He came from Lorca, Spain, to Chamita, New Mexico. Chamita is near Española. From there the family settled in Questa.

I would like to know more about Judaism. Father said, "Keep your heritage because it is very important to know where you came from. Keep the traditions."

# APPENDIX

## JUDAISM IN MEMORY AND SPIRIT, 500 YEARS AFTER THE SPANISH AND PORTUGUESE INQUISITIONS, WHAT REMNANTS OF JUDAISM REMAIN?

Information and definitions offered in the appendix confirm Jewish practices or vestiges of Jewish practices mentioned in the oral histories.

### Anusim

"Involuntary converts—those under physical duress or fear, etc.—are *anusim*, literally 'forced ones.' The distinction was very important to many rabbis in determining whether those who came from Spain or Portugal during the reign of the Holy Office to communities where religious freedom existed should be accepted as Jews without any ceremony."[1]

"In 1497, Jews in Portugal were ordered to leave or convert, but children were prohibited from leaving. They were to be forcibly converted. Most parents opted to convert in order to retain their children. These people are known as the *anusim* (Heb., forced ones). Many of the *anusim* or their descendants ultimately migrated to the New World."[2]

### Ashkenazim

"Literally, Germans. The name was applied to Jews of Germany and Northern France beginning in the 10th century. In the middle of the 16th century, the term Ashkenazim came to include Jews of Eastern Europe as well. The Ashkenazim have developed a set of distinctive customs and rituals, different from those of the Sephardim, that is, Jews from Spain, Portugal, Mediterranean countries, and North Africa."[3]

**Gloria Golden**

### *Auto-da-fé*

"Literally, Act of Faith. It was a religious ceremony. There were different kinds: *auto particular* or *autillo*, which was for light offenses and could be private or held within convent grounds, without outsiders present; and *auto general* or *auto público general* held as a *fiesta* day, when a public holiday was declared and attendance was practically mandatory for all within miles around, including the Indians. Not all the penitents at these *autos general* went to the stake. Those who recanted in time recited the most debasing confessions, holding a candle in each hand. Decrees for less than capital punishment were read aloud and *sambenitos* donned."[4]

"*Sanbenito*; a penitent's garb depicting the 'crime(s)' committed by the individual."[5]

### *Avoid Blood*

"Because Leviticus 17:11 states that 'the life of the flesh is in the blood,' kosher rules prohibit the consumption of blood."[6]

Elvira Cunha de Azevedo Mea, in *Sentencas da Inquisicão de Coimbra em metropolitanos de D. Frei Bartolomeu dos Mártires* (1567-1582), explains: "Filipa Fernándes, of Seia [Coimbra 1583], allegedly 'washed in the Jewish fashion the meat that came from the butcher shop in order to remove all the blood because eating it was a sin'" (qtd. in Gitlitz 546-47).[7]

### *Baking*

"Throwing a piece of the bread dough into the fire before it was shaped for baking was a widespread custom among the Jewish women. It is a universal practice of Orthodox women who bake their own bread. There is a statement in the *Mishna*, the book of commentaries and interpretations of the *Torah*, *Bame Madlikin*, to the effect that a woman may die for any one of three transgressions. One is for 'failing to separate the *challah*.' The act of throwing a piece of dough into the fire is symbolic of the sacrifices during the time of the Temple in Jerusalem." [8]

"There are even echoes of the custom among modern crypto-Jews. [Samuel] Schwarz [explains in *Os Cristãos-novos em Portugal no século XX* that he] found twentieth-century Portuguese Judaizers throwing a bit of their *matza* dough into the fire" (qtd. in Gitlitz 548-49).[9]

### Bar Mitzvah

"Literally, 'son of the Commandment'; a boy who has reached the age of thirteen and is expected to accept adult religious responsibilities. The female equivalent of *Bar Mitzvah* is called *Bat Mitzvah*. This 'coming of age' is the occasion for a ritual in the synagogue, where on the first *Sabbath* of his fourteenth year, the boy is called for the first time to read from the *Torah* and the prophets. It is a joyous occasion, accompanied by gifts for the *Bar Mitzvah* boy from friends and family. Traditionally, the *Bar Mitzvah* boy delivers a learned speech. . . . The beginnings of this ceremony are ancient. References to the custom are found as early as the 5th and 6th centuries."[10]

"In 1989 Anne Cardoza [in her book, *I am a Marrano*,] reported that her Grandmother, Pauline, who emigrated from Gerona to Buenos Aires to the United States, advised her children to 'share the family secret with adult children over age 13'" (qtd. in Gitlitz 223). [11]

### Basque

"One of a people of unknown origin inhabiting the western Pyrenees regions in France and Spain."[12]

According to research in the Basque region, Myrna Katz Frommer and Harvey Frommer were told that the Jews have occupied the Basque area for centuries. Although they never attained the same level of distinction as Jews living elsewhere in "medieval Spain," the Jews in the Basque region were not affected by the same degree of anti-Semitism. As indicated in the article, the Jews were afforded greater protection in this area because the Inquisition was not active there. The Jewish population was about "60,000" at one time, and there are about "10,000" at present. The Basques have a saying: "We know who the Jews are because we used to be Jews." The people are aware that Judaism is the foundation of Christianity. [13]

### Blessings

"A *berakhah* (blessing) is a special kind of prayer that is very common in Judaism."[14]

"For the observant Spanish male Jew prior to the Expulsion, almost every routine daily activity was sanctified by prayer. Jews prayed when they first arose in the morning, at mid-day, and when they went to bed. . . . They blessed their children. They prayed when they left their houses and murmured another prayer when they entered again."[15]

"Fragments of prayers are scattered throughout Inquisition documents in both Spain and Portugal. They were recorded in large numbers in Portugal from the 1570s onward, largely because at that time the Portuguese Inquisition introduced questions about prayers into their protocol of interrogation."[16]

"*Converso* or crypto-Jewish parents would bless their children, especially when they were leaving the house, perhaps to move or get married. The children would kneel, and the parents would place two hands on their heads. They would then place the sign of the cross on their foreheads in case someone saw."[17]

"The following . . . [practice is] revealed in the Admonitions (methods by which to detect Jews) of the inquisitor general's office in Lisbon, November 1536. . . . 12. They place their hands on the heads of their children when blessing them but do not make the sign of the Cross. (This was the basis for the conviction of Ana Roiz, who was taken to Lisbon, convicted there, and burned at the stake in 1593.)"[18]

"Among the most long-lived were the blessings (*Birkat ha-bonim*) that parents uttered over their children. An early compilation of Judaizing customs described this blessing in its most basic form: 'They put their hand on top of the head, drawing it down over the face without making the sign of the cross, which they say recalls the blessing that Jacob gave to Menasseh and Ephraim, his grandchildren, sons of Joseph born in Egypt, when he put his hands on their heads and blessed him as is written at the end of Genesis in the testament of Jacob.' Testimony in hundreds of cases suggests that this was a very accurate description."[19]

### Before Meals

"Benedictions are said before eating any food or drinking any beverage. Each benediction begins with the words: *baruch atah adonai elokeinu melech haolam.* The ending depends on what is to be eaten or drunk."[20]

According to Ramón Santa María, in his book, *La Inquisición de Ciudad-Real; Proceso original del difunto Juan Martínez de los Olivos,* "In a 1484 trial in Ciudad Real it was reported that *conversos* 'blessed the bread in the Jewish fashion, and then blessed a glass of wine'" (qtd. in Gitlitz 452).[21]

### After Meals

"One of the most important prayers, one of the very few that the Bible commands us to recite, is never recited in synagogue. That prayer is *birkat ha-mazon*, grace after meals.

In Deuteronomy 8, 10, we are commanded that when we eat and are satisfied, we must bless the LORD, our God. This commandment is fulfilled by reciting the *birkat ha-mazon* (blessing of the food) after each meal."[22]

Abraham E. Millgram, in his book, *Jewish Worship*, explains: "The much more elaborate traditional prayers following the meal thank God in turn for the food which has just been consumed, the gift of the land of Israel, the rebuilding of Jerusalem (no matter that it still lay in ruins), and for preserving Judaism from destruction. The grace after meals is alluded to frequently in Inquisition testimony" (qtd. in Gitlitz 452).[23]

### Bread and Wine

"Bread and wine . . . because of their importance in Jewish tradition a special prayer was assigned to them. No *Sabbath* or holiday meal and no special party meal (*seuda*) is considered complete without bread and wine. Their distinction has been linked to Scripture, which speaks of bread as the food that sustains life and wine as the food that adds joy to life (Psalms 104:14-15)."[24]

### Buñuelos

"Nowadays these honeyed puff fritters, because they are fried in olive oil, are a *Hanukah* tradition among Sephardic communities all around the Mediterranean, where they are generally called *bimuelos*. However, *Hanukah*, judging from Inquisition testimonies and from other documents relating to the Jews, seems to have been an extremely minor holiday in late medieval Iberia, for references to its celebration are exceedingly rare. Instead the puff fritters seem to have been associated with a number of other holidays, including Passover and *Yom Kippur*, as well as festive family celebrations. Margarita de Rivera's family in Mexico in 1643 considered the consumption of 'fritters and honey' an essential part of the wedding ceremony."[25]

"The establishment of seven days (*shiva* means 'seven' in Hebrew) as the first and most intense stage of mourning is based on an interpretation of a verse of Amos (8:10): 'And I will turn your feasts [which usually lasted seven days] into mourning, and all your songs into lamentations; and I will bring sackcloth upon all loins, and baldness upon every head; and I will make it as the mourning for an only son; and the end thereof is a bitter day.'

"The Rabbis interpret the words of Amos to mean that just as feasts (Passover, *Sukkot*, etc.) were celebrated for seven days, so must the initial period of mourning last seven (*shiva*) days."[26]

According to the Archivo Histórico Nacional in Madrid, "Once the body is ritually clean, it should be clothed in a shroud. . . . The shroud is a very simple garb of muslin, linen, or cotton, usually white and without pockets; it is made by hand, and women obviously sewed the shrouds in addition to placing them on the bodies of the deceased. The judaizers were concerned with having proper shrouds made for them and occasionally left instructions to that effect on their deathbeds."[27]

"[In the New World] upon the demise of a family member, the cadaver was douched thoroughly and dressed in a shroud of new linen, preferably from Rouen, France. After 1620, linen from Holland was considered equal to that of Rouen. The choice of the particular places for the manufacture of the linen originates with the biblical injunction against wearing material made of more than one kind of fiber. Rouen had Jewish linen manufacturers as did Holland when it became an alternate source, and their products were considered pure."[28]

"To leave a body unburied for an extended period of time is considered disrespectful; therefore, in keeping with the principle of *k'vod ha-met*, Judaism mandates that burial should take place as soon as possible after the death, preferably within 24 hours."[29]

According to the Archivo Histórico Nacional in Madrid, "Once the body was buried (and the *conversos* did not have the luxury of burying their dead in a Jewish cemetery), the mourners returned home, accompanied by friends and family, and partook of the traditional post burial meal, known as the *cohuerzo*. . . . Constanza Díaz [Castilian Conversa] admitted not only to sitting *shiva* (observing the seven days of mourning) and to eating the traditional meatless meal when she was in mourning, but to sending food to the home of other mourners at appropriate times. The mourner, forbidden to work, cannot even prepare his or her meals; other members of the family or community must provide the food."[30]

Joshua Trachtenberg, in *Jewish Magic and Superstition*, states: "Some superstitions were derived from the *Kabbala*, the source of Jewish mysticism since the twelfth century. Throwing soil on the coffin while it is being lowered into the grave is still practiced. The use of virgin soil, especially if it came from the Holy Land, is believed to prevent the soul from returning to the earth and to encourage its ascent to heaven. Some believed that the soul does not wish to depart this terrestrial sphere" (qtd. in Liebman 101).[31]

"When the body of the deceased is lowered into the grave, it is customary that anyone present may participate in covering the grave with earth. Reason: The *Torah* (*Devarim* 13:5) states: 'Follow *Hashem* your God.' The *Gemara* (*Sotah* 14a) asks: Is it possible for a human being to truly follow the Divine presence? The real intent is that we should emulate the attributes of God. Just as He clothes the naked so shall we....Just as God buries the dead [as it says: 'And He buried him in the valley' (*Devarim* 34:6)] similarly you too should [emulate the compassionate attributes of *Hashem* and] bury the dead (*Keser Shem Tov*).[32]

"Mirrors [are] covered in a house of mourning. . . . The

most popular explanation is that mirrors are associated with personal vanity. During a period of mourning, it is not appropriate to be concerned with one's personal appearance."[33]

"[It is] considered an obligation to pay a condolence call to mourners during the first week of mourning. Paying a condolence visit is an act of compassion often theologically connected with God's message to the Jewish people as expressed by the prophet Isaiah: 'Comfort ye, comfort ye, my people' (40:1). The condolence call during the *Shiva* period helps the mourner through his initial period of depression and loneliness."[34]

"A tombstone [is] erected over the grave of the deceased. According to scholars, this practice dates back to biblical times. When Rachel died on the road to Bethlehem, Jacob 'set up a pillar upon her grave' (Genesis 35:20)."[35]

"There is a theory among scholars that the first tombstones were erected in the Middle Ages, when many people believed in ghosts. A grave was promptly filled with earth so as to contain the ghost of the deceased, who might otherwise harm his enemies. And the tombstone was originally employed for the same purpose."[36]

"[Stones are placed] on the tombstone when visiting the gravesite. This is a symbolic act indicating that members of the family and friends have not forgotten the deceased."[37]

"Preparation by neighbors of the first full meal eaten by mourners after returning from the funeral is a very old Jewish tradition. The Rabbis of the *Talmudic* period reprimanded neighbors who were so callous that they did not prepare food for a neighbor who was burying his dead, thus displaying a lack of concern for a neighbor's grief."[38]

"Jewish law...looks with disfavor upon embalming, unless extenuating circumstances exist. Embalming sometimes involves mutilation of the body, an act of irreverence toward the dead."[39]

"In embalming, the blood is drained from the body and discarded. Jewish law regards the blood as part of the body; it must not be removed from the deceased.

"The embalming of Jacob and Joseph, mentioned in the Bible, was an Egyptian custom. Embalming was not a prevalent practice among Jews."[40]

### Capirotada

"Another Lenten/Passover food is 'capirotada'. It's wheat bread (pilon-cillo) to which raw sugar, cinnamon, cheese, butter, pecans, peanuts and raisins are added. These are identical ingredients to those used by secret Spanish Jews in the New Spain of 1640 to make their breads and cakes. Even the ingredients and recipes have been recorded by the Holy Office of the Inquisition and saved to this day in the archives."[41]

See also **Panocha**

### Carvajal

"Trials beginning in the late 1570s reveal a well-established, well-networked, observant (in their fashion) Judaizing community centered in Mexico City. In 1579 Luis de Carvajal, a thoroughly assimilated new-Christian adventurer, was given a royal patent to exploit and govern a vast area called Nuevo León, which is now the entire northeast corner of the country of Mexico. Among his family were several clergymen and a Portuguese captain-general. Also among the many dozens of extended family members who accompanied him were some active crypto-Jews. Attracted to the Carvajal group, perhaps because the royal patent for exploration and settlement of this region omitted the requirement that immigrants present a certificate of purity-of-blood, were many other crypto-Jews from Spain, Portugal, and other parts of Europe. This large group formed the backbone of late sixteenth-century Mexican crypto-Judaism. Their trials during the 1580s and 1590s constitute our best window on colonial crypto-Judaism at that time. The governor, Luis de Carvajal the Elder, who was found guilty not of Judaizing but of abetting heresy, died in disgrace. His nephew, Luis de Carvajal the Younger, the mystic visionary, poet, and fervently observant Judaizer, was tried in 1589 and 1595-6 and eventually burned as an unrepentant heretic."[42]

### Circumcision

"Performed upon the Jewish male child on the eighth day of life. In Genesis 17:10-14, God commands Abraham to circumcise the foreskin of all males of the house as the sign of the covenant between God and the children of Abraham. It has become a basic law among Jews. In times of persecution, Jews risked their lives to fulfill the commandment."[43]

"Because circumcision was such an important emblem of commitment to Judaizing, it drew a great deal of attention from Inquisitors. Consequently, we know in considerable detail how circumcisions were performed by those Judaizers in later generations who retained the custom. For knowledgeable Judaizers the ceremony was not unlike that performed even today in normative Judaism."[44]

"The Edict of Expulsion emphasized the belief that instruction was provided by the Jews to the conversos, especially at gatherings. These Jews supposedly induced the New Christians to circumcise their sons, gave them books, told them when to fast, and instructed them in their law."[45]

### Columbus

"There is evidence that Columbus spoke Spanish while still living in Italy, an unusual situation unless his family had originated in Spain.  Spanish-speaking Jewish refugees from the Inquisition were numerous in the Genoa area.

"The form 'Colon' which Columbus adopted as the Spanish equivalent of his last name was not the expected form (which would have been 'Colom' or 'Colombo').  It was however a common Jewish variation on the name.

"Columbus was known to frequent the company of Jews and former Jews, among whom were some noted astronomers and navigators, as well as his official translator. *Marranos* figure prominently among Columbus's backers and crew."[46]

*Ancestors Mentioned by Carlos Casaus*

According to an article on Bartolomé De Las Casas, he was "born in Seville [1484] to Pedro de Las Casas" who had the means to educate his son in Seville .[47]

Bartholomé was a priest whose "father, Pedro de Las Casas, and three uncles" came to the New World with "Christopher Columbus on his second voyage" in the year 1493.[48]

The grandparents of Bartolomé de Las Casas (1474-1566) "were all baptized Christians, but his paternal grandparents were of the Jewish *converso* Peñalosa family of Seville."[49]

### *Conversos*

"Many Spanish Jews converted to Catholicism in the late fourteenth and fifteenth centuries, especially in the aftermath of the Edict of Expulsion in 1492.  These '*conversos*,' often called 'New Christians,' included many who became devout, believing Catholics, or at any rate educated their children to be.  Others, however, preserved Jewish practices and did their utmost to retain some sort of Jewish identity. Most knew little or nothing about the Jewish religion and beliefs of their ancestors; some may have developed an interest in Judaism only after threatened by or actually charged by the Inquisition."[50]

### Covering Heads (Women)

"In early *Talmudic* times, it became common practice for married women to keep their heads covered. Rabbi Sheshet said, 'A woman's hair is sexually exciting.' To be out of doors with head uncovered was a serious breach of law and custom, and it constituted sufficient grounds for a man to divorce his wife without being required to pay her any of the monies normally due upon divorce, as stipulated in the marriage contract."[51]

"The Code of Jewish Law states: 'Married women always keep their heads covered; unmarried women do not have to keep their heads covered.' The purpose of the legislation is to make perfectly clear to men the marital status of a woman."[52]

"In biblical times women covered their heads with scarves or veils as a sign of chastity and modesty. To expose a woman's hair was considered a humiliation (Numbers 5:18)."[53]

Liebman, in his book, *The Inquisitors and the Jews in the New World: Summaries of Procesos, 1500-1810, and Bibliographic Guide*, gives the following account: "Francisco López Díaz [1648] confessed that he had attended a synagogue in Seville where 'the men prayed wearing hats and the women wore large headdresses' " (qtd. in Gitlitz 528). [54]

### Crypto-Jew

"Practicing Jews who publicly pretended to be Catholic."[55]

"The Jews in the Spanish New World were known as crypto-Jews; *hebreo-cristianos* (Hebrew Christians); *conversos* (converts); *nuevos-cristianos* (New Christians); and Portuguese. The Holy Office officials never used the word '*Marrano*.'"[56]

### Dreidel

"The dreidel originated around 175 B.C. This would have been during the persecution of the Jews, under the Seleucid King Antiochus IV. He was commonly known as 'Epimanes' the 'Mad One,' a play on his official title 'Epiphanes,' the 'Divinely Manifest.' He banned study of *Torah* and worship in the Temple. Antiochus attempted to introduce pagan rites in Jerusalem. He ordered all holy books confiscated and burned. The Jews of ancient Judea continued to pray and study *Torah* in secret. During these study sessions, small spinning tops were kept on the table top. If Antioch's soldiers entered the house, the holy books were hidden. Everyone pretended to be playing a simple gambling game with small tops, thereby averting disaster.

"As a result of persecution under the Spanish and Portuguese Inquisitions, many Jews went underground and continued to practice Judaism in secret. Some of the children played with a 4-sided spinning top called a '*trompos*,' similar to a dreidel. On the sides were written in Spanish 'take all,' 'put back,' 'take one' and 'nothing.' Compare to the dreidel: *Nun* (nothing), *Gimmel* (all), *Shin* (put in one)and *He* (take half). Some of these customs are said to be typical of Hispanics in the Southwestern United States, whose ancestors went north to avoid the Inquisition."[57]

According to a response from María on saudades-sefared@yahoogroups.com, "Both my parents used to play with them, and so did I. My Mother thought it was just a children's toy in Portugal. I don't know what my Dad thought, because he is no longer here. In Portugal we play by spinning, and the letters are written as RTDP—R = *Rapa* (meaning takes all), T=*Tira* (take it), D=*Deixa* (leave it), and P=*Poe* (put back-no play). It took me years in the States to figure out it was a Jewish tradition and used during a particular holiday."[58]

Temple Emanuel of Cleveland, Ohio explains *Chanukah* Traditions. The Dreidel: "The word 'dreidel' comes from the German word *dreihen* (to spin). The dreidel was a popular toy in medieval Germany. Historians claim that the dreidel was originally a 3-sided top used as a German Christmas toy. The game itself is not German in origin, but rather, the Germans borrowed the game from the Greeks and Romans."[59]

### *Edict of Expulsion (The Alhambra Decree)*

"This is the decree of expulsion promulgated by Queen Isabella and King Ferdinand of Spain in 1492, which forced the Spanish Jews, the Sephardim, to leave Spain forever. . . . You well know that in our dominion, there are certain bad Christians that judaized and committed apostasy against our Holy Catholic faith, much of it the cause of communications between Jews and Christians. Therefore, in the year 1480, we ordered that the Jews be separated from the cities and towns of our domains and that they be given separate quarters, hoping that by such separation the situation would be remedied. And we ordered that and an Inquisition be established in such domains; and in twelve years it has functioned, the Inquisition has found many guilty persons.

"Furthermore, we are informed by the Inquisition and others that the great harm done to the Christians persists, and it continues because of the conversations and communications that they have with the Jews, such Jews trying by whatever manner to subvert our holy Catholic faith and trying to draw faithful Christians away from their beliefs.

"These Jews instruct these Christians in the ceremonies and observances of their Law, circumcising their children, and giving them books with which to pray, and declaring unto them the days of fasting, and meeting with them to teach them the histories of their Law. . . . Therefore, with the council and advice of the eminent men and cavaliers of our reign, and of other persons of knowledge and conscience of our Supreme Council, after much deliberation, it is agreed and resolved that all Jews and Jewesses be ordered to leave our kingdoms, and that they never be allowed to return."[60]

### Education

"In many ways, Jewish history is the story of the education of a people. From the beginning, many great Jewish leaders were also great teachers who spoke to the world through the Jewish people. When the world's mystery and wonder were fresh in the human mind, the patriarch Abraham thought about its mystery and wondered about its Creator. He discarded his father's idols and began to teach his tribe to believe in one God. Thus, the founder of the Jewish people was also the first teacher in Jewish history. Moses, the Lawgiver who led the people to freedom, was called *rabbenu*, our teacher. He taught the children of Israel during their years of wandering, and he designated times when the people should come together and study. When the Children of Israel settled in the Promised Land and were ruled by judges, there were no schools, so knowledge was handed down by word of mouth from father to son, mother to daughter."[61]

"Education came to be of utmost importance in the life of the people. After the destruction of the Second Temple by the Romans, the rabbis taught that study, like prayer, was a form of worship and a substitute for sacrifices. During the *Talmudic* period in Babylonia, the rabbis set up a complete, lifelong system of education that began at the age of five or six."[62]

"The education system begun in Palestine and developed in Babylonia moved with the people wherever they went. By the 11th century, persecution and intolerance had driven the Jews out of Babylonia. The great centers dwindled and almost disappeared, and Jews set up new communities in Spain, Italy, France, and Germany."[63]

"During the Middle Ages, when even princes and nobles were illiterate, the Jewish community had many scholars and honored them above other men."[64]

### Empanadas

Empanadas were quite popular during medieval times in Europe. They were eaten by most people including the Jews and conversos of Iberia. The empanadas are "pies or pastries" that contained "meat, vegetables, and fish" for the filling. [65]

"The traditional empanada is a six inch turnover filled with either sweet yam or pumpkin. Apple, peach or pineapple can also be used as filler. . . . The smaller empanadita usually measures about three to four inches as a finished product. The empanaditas of New Mexico and turcos of South Texas are one and the same. They are the traditional Jewish knishes, meat filled turnovers."[66]

### Endogamy

"Conversos tended to prefer other conversos as spouses for several reasons. For some it was a matter of business: They hoped to keep family money and property within the converso enclave. Much more important, those families which were struggling to keep the Jewish traditions vital and who lived with the Inquisition looking over their shoulders were extremely reluctant to run the risk of having an 'outsider' scrutinize their religious practices and perhaps disclose the Judaizing (or allegedly Judaizing) customs of converso members."[67]

### Fasting

"One of the customs the crypto-Jews kept, in order to

attain redemption and expiate their guilt for conversion to Catholicism, was fasting. Although Jewish law mandates fasting only on *Yom Kippur*, Mexican Jews fasted several times during the year. People also had to keep their fasting from servants. One tactic was to send servants away on errands during mealtimes, when the food was thrown away."[68]

"After *Yom Kippur*, the most important fasting occasion was *Purim*, a holiday which celebrated Queen Esther and her confession of her faith to her husband, the King, in order to save the Jews."[69]

### Halakhah

"Judaism is not just a set of *beliefs* about God, man and the universe. Judaism is a comprehensive way of life, filled with rules and practices that affect every aspect of life: what you do when you wake up in the morning, what you can and cannot *eat*, what you can and cannot wear, how to groom yourself, how to conduct business, who you can *marry*, how to observe the *holidays* and *Sabbaths*, and perhaps most important, how to behave towards God, *other people*, and *animals*. This set of rules and practices is known as *halakhah*."[70]

"At the heart of *halakhah* is the unchangeable 613 *mitzvot* that God gave to the Jewish people in the *Torah* (the first five books of the Bible). The word '*mitzvah*' means commandment. . . . Some of the *mitzvot* are clear, explicit commands in the Bible (thou shalt not murder; to write words of *Torah* on the *doorposts* of your house), others are more implicit (the *mitzvah* to recite *grace after meals*, which is inferred from 'and you will eat and be satisfied and bless the LORD your God'), and some can only be ascertained by *Talmudic* logic (that a man shall not commit incest with his daughter, which is derived from the commandment not to commit incest with his daughter's daughter)."[71]

See also *Mitzvot*

## Hanukkah

"The Feast of Dedication and Lights, which falls on the 25th of Kislev and lasts for eight days. It marks the rededication of the Temple by Judah Maccabee in 165 B.C.E. after his victory over the Syrians who had defiled the sanctuary. Tradition relates that Judah could find only a single cruse of oil which had not been contaminated by the enemy. Although it contained only enough oil to light the menorah for one day, a miracle took place, and it burned for eight. Therefore, candles are lit throughout the holiday, one on the eve of the first day, two on the eve of the second, and so forth, until eight are kindled on the last evening."[72]

According to Ramón Santa María, in his book, *Ritos y costumbres de los hebreos españoles,* "Although the festival of *Hanukkah* has assumed major importance in twentieth-century Western culture, probably because of its close proximity to Christmas, it appears to have been of minor significance in pre- or post-Expulsion Iberia. There are a few references from around the time of the Expulsion to Spanish Jews celebrating the holiday. Only two pre-Expulsion Spanish *Hanukkah* lamps are known to survive. A memorandum prepared for Inquisitors in the late fifteenth century says that Judaizers 'celebrate the Feast of Candles and they light them one at a time up to ten, and then they blow them out; and they pray Jewish prayers' " (qtd. in Gitlitz 376).[73]

### Inquisition

"The special courts set up by the Catholic Church to check the spread of heretical opinion among the faithful, first formed in the 13th century. It was most active, however, in Spain, where it began in 1480. In time, the dreaded activities of this agency of the Church came to be directed mainly at ferreting out the *Marranos,* Jews who had been forcibly converted to Christianity and were found secretly observing the practices of Judaism.

"It is estimated that in 350 years of Inquisition activities (roughly from 1480 to 182l), about 400,000 Jews were brought before these ecclesiastical tribunals; 30,000 were put to death. Punishment was carried out in public squares to serve both as a warning and a demonstration of 'the glory of the Church.' Hence, an inquisitorial execution was known as *auto-da-fé*, an act of faith."[74]

"There were six hundred thousand to one million *conversos* in Spain at the time, representing about 7 percent of the total population."[75]

According to Juan Antonio Llorente, in his book, *Histoire Critique de l'Inquisition d'Espagne*, "By December 1482, two thousand women and men had been burned in Seville, two thousand more had been burned in effigy, and seventeen thousand had been 'reconciled' with varying degrees of punishment. . . . *Conversos* were objects of a nationwide hunt, the focus of an exploding racist consciousness masquerading under the cloak of religion" (qtd. in Paris 166).[76]

### Jewish Saints

"[An] example of syncretism was the late adoption by crypto-Jewish communities of a set of 'Jewish saints' similar to Christian saints in their ability to work miracles and intercede with the deity. Moses figured large in this slate, as did Esther: their popularity derived from the fact that they each were seen as the savior of the Jewish people from alien religious oppression."[77]

### Judaizing

"Practicing Judaism secretly. . . . That a large number of Brazil's colonizers were judaizers is a fact Inquisition trial records make abundantly clear. One must keep in mind that the simple act of bathing on Fridays could be construed as 'a lapse into Judaism', setting in motion an inquest certain to end badly for the accused."[78]

## Kaddish

"One of the most ancient prayers in the Jewish prayer book, generally recited in the synagogue during religious services. It became popular as the mourner's prayer. . . . The mourner's *Kaddish* is recited at synagogue services for eleven months and on every anniversary of the relative's death."[79]

"Prior to the Expulsion crypto-Jews might even contract with openly practicing Jews to recite the *Kaddish* in their stead for their departed relatives or even for themselves. . . . As with many *converso* rituals, this one evolved over the centuries as the traditional prayers were forgotten and *conversos* composed others to take their place. One of the most complete prayers was preserved in the Mexican archives when in 1642 Rafael de Granada recalled for Inquisitors—in somewhat garbled fashion—a mourning prayer his mother María de Rivera had taught him, which was to be recited during the Wednesday fasts for the souls of the departed."[80]

## Kashrut

"Observance of the laws of *kashrut* has been a unifying factor for the Jewish people throughout the ages, continually serving to remind Jews of their roots.

"The primary dietary laws are set forth in the Book of Leviticus, where a list of kosher and nonkosher animals is given. The rationale for these laws is not elucidated. The Bible merely states that the laws be observed because 'I am the Lord that brought you up out of the land of Egypt, to be your God. Ye shall therefore be holy, for I am holy' (Leviticus 11:44).

"Holiness is the only reason given in the Bible for the observance of the dietary laws."[81]

"The Bible reiterates many times that blood may not be consumed because blood symbolizes the very essence and distinctiveness of man (Leviticus 3:17 and Deuteronomy 13:23-25). Based on this, the Rabbis of the *Talmud* concluded that when an animal is killed for food, care must be taken that as much blood as possible is drained off before eating the meat.

"When an animal is slaughtered in accordance with Jewish ritual law, the jugular vein is severed, the animal dies instantaneously, and the maximum amount of blood leaves the body."[82]

"The religious [belief] of the Jews of the late sixteenth and most of the seventeenth century. . . . [is that] one must not eat pork or anything of the pig. Only flesh of animals that chew the cud is permitted. Fish without scales are prohibited. All fowl must be decapitated and the blood drained from them and from all animals to be eaten. No animal blood or suet may be eaten."[83]

"The method of [ritual] slaughter is a quick, deep stroke across the throat with a perfectly sharp blade with no nicks or unevenness. This method is painless, causes unconsciousness within seconds, and is widely recognized as the most humane method of slaughter possible. . . . [It] ensures rapid, complete draining of the blood."[84]

"The thigh vein and surrounding suet was always removed. The removal of the vein was called *landrecilla* (porging). This practice often resulted in the exposure of a Jew. Hindquarters were discarded."[85]

Ramón Santa María, in his book, *Ritos y costumbres de los hebreos españoles*, informs us: "As explained in the late fifteenth century, 'removing the sciatic vein from the legs of cattle, before they are cooked, is in remembrance of when the Angel fought with Jacob and he was left lame; and because of this the children of Israel do not eat the nerve in the leg nor the fat which is connected to it, which is the sciatic vein, as is written at the end of Genesis' " (qtd. in Gitlitz 547).[86]

According to Rafael de Lera García, in his book, *La última gran persecución inquisitorial contra el criptojudaísmo: el Tribunal de Cuenca, 1718-1725*, "Jews and most Judaizing *conversos* shunned animals that had been killed by strangling, which was the normal practice among Christians. In fact, as late as 1720 an *auto de fé* in Madrid identified twenty families whose Judaizing included abstaining from eating foul that had been slaughtered by strangling.

"Kosher butchers [according to Santa María] routinely covered the spilled blood with dirt or with ashes. . . . [According to Ángela Selke de Sánchez, in her book, *Los Chuetas y la Inquisición: Vida y muerte en el ghetto de Mallorca,*] In 1688 someone called '*la Moyaneta*' explained the custom this way: 'blood was the animals' soul, and therefore God ordered it to be covered' " (qtd. in Gitlitz 545).[87]

Santa María further states: "Jews bury the blood of the fowl they slaughter because it is a commandment of their law, and because the blood of fowl was not customarily used for sacrifice to God, as was the blood of other animals, as is written in the third of the five books of Moses."[88]

"[Richard Santos'] grandfather, a chef by trade, killed fowl in two different manners. . . . The 'chicken killing knives' were different from the 'meat slicing knives' which were different from the 'vegetable knives'. When on the field as a chef for H. B. Zachry (highway construction) Company, Manuel Almeida usually killed chickens by wringing off the neck. . . . One grabs a chicken (or turkey) by the neck and whirls it about until the fowl is decapitated. The fowl is then hung upside down and its blood is allowed to drip into a tin can or hole in the ground."[89]

The method of killing chickens in the Southwest may be related to the *Kapparot* ritual, explained as follows:

"*Kapparot* is a custom in which the sins of a person are symbolically transferred to a fowl. It is practiced by some Jews shortly before *Yom Kippur*. First, selections from Isaiah 11:9, Psalms 107:10, 14, and 17-21, and Job 33:23-24 are recited; then a rooster (for a male) or a hen (for a female) is held above the person's head and swung in a circle three times, while the following is spoken: 'This is my exchange, my substitute, my atonement; this rooster (or hen) shall go to its death, but I shall go to a good, long life, and to peace.' The hope is that the fowl, which is then donated to the poor for food, will take on any misfortune that might otherwise occur to the one who has taken part in the ritual, in punishment for his or her sins."[90]

### Separation of Meat and Dairy

"On three separate occasions, the *Torah* tells us not to 'boil a kid in its mother's milk' (Exodus 23,19; Exodus 34,26; Deuteronomy 14,21). The *Oral Torah* explains that this passage prohibits eating meat and dairy together. . . . This separation includes not only the foods themselves, but the utensils, pots and pans with which they are cooked, the plates and flatware from which they are eaten, the dishwashers or dishpans in wish they are cleaned, and the towels on which they are dried."[91]

### Key-the Key from Spain

"According to legend, when the Jews were expelled from Spain in 1492, they took with them the keys to their homes and synagogues hoping that one day they would return. They never did, but their Spanish cultural heritage remained a powerful influence in their lives."[92]

"My grandmother used to keep all her keys, and there were so many. I don't know where they all came from. I have most of them now. I don't know why she had that custom. I read that the people who left Portugal and Spain long ago, used to take their keys with them in their journey of the unknowns, in hope of returning one day. The Mayor of Castelo de Vide told us that descendants of those who left had returned to visit the town of their ancestors, bringing with them drawings and keys that the ancestors had handed down from generation to generation. It was interesting that even the house of the midwife was drawn on a map."[93]

### Laco Ritual (Wedding Rituals)

"[A wedding ritual among the secret Jews of Portugal is] to bind the bride and groom's hands with a white cloth while a prayer is said."[94]

"Few of these customs have survived into modern times except in Portugal, where several two-ceremony weddings—a Catholic church wedding and a Jewish wedding replete with rings and the blessings of Abraham, Isaac, and Jacob—have been reported. [Samuel] Schwarz, [in his book, *Os Cristãos-novos em Portugal no século XX*], describes one of these weddings. Several days before the civil ceremony the bride and groom, each with two friends, stood among their families. A family member joined their hands, bound them with a linen cloth, and pronounced a blessing: 'In the name of the God of Abraham, Isaac and Jacob, I join you into one. May you fulfill His benediction.' To judge from other reports, the most important aspect of this ceremony was the joining of new spouses' hands" (qtd. in Gitlitz 257).[95]

### Lactose Intolerance

"Persons with lactose intolerance lack sufficient amounts of the enzyme lactase, which breaks down lactose or milk sugar. When milk products are consumed, the lactose remains undigested in the intestine; in some people, it then causes gastrointestinal pain, bloating, cramps, flatulence and diarrhea."[96]

"Population groups displaying proportions of lactose malabsorption (80-100%) are generally found in geographic areas in which dairying or adult milk usage has never, until perhaps recently, been a part of the culture. In the absence of genetic challenge, no evolution has occurred. These areas include the majority of the world's population; American Indians and Eskimos; most Mediterranean and Near Eastern groups. . . . Finally, a small group in the mid-range of lactose malabsorption prevalence (30-60%) is found to be dominated by populations whose ancestry is mixed-absorbers (milk users) and malabsorbers. These include: some American Blacks, African Arab mixes, Eskimo-Finnish people, and Mexican-Americans among others (Simmons, F.J. 1978)."[97]

### Ladino

"(Judeo-Spanish). When the Jews left Spain in 1492, the Spanish language was on the verge of change. The old form is preserved today only in the Jewish dialect called Ladino. It is also called Spaniolish or Castiliano. It is spoken by Sephardic Jews in Turkey, the Balkans, part of North Africa, in Israel, and the Americas. . . . From the beginning, Ladino included Hebrew words. Later, it picked up Arabic, Turkish, Greek, French, and Italian words."[98]

### Magen David

"Literally, shield of David. The six-cornered star made by overlapping two triangles is an ancient and widespread symbol. Many ancient architectural ruins carry the engraving of this Hebrew seal. The 3rd- or 4th-century synagogue dug up in Capernaum, Israel, has not only the six-pointed Magen David upon it, but also the rarer five-pointed Seal of Solomon."[99]

### Marrano

"The Holy Office officials never used the word 'Marrano.'"[100]

"Marrano, meaning 'hog' or 'swine,' is included in government records as early as 965. Antonio Domínguez

Ortiz reports that in the thirteenth century it was a criminal offense punished by a fine and jail to call a person a *marrano*. . . . By the late fourteenth century, the word assumed a pejorative sense. By the fifteenth century, it was applied by Jews to other Jews who became sincere converts to Christianity."[101]

### Masons

"Eight men created the Grand Lodge of Masons in New Mexico one mid-summer day in 1877. . . . New Mexico had become a part of the United States at the close of the war with Mexico thirty years earlier. While there had been a few Americans in the territory before 1846, at the time the Grand Lodge was formed there were still only a few thousand who had come to this new and rugged country from the states. Perhaps ninety percent of those residing in the area were of Mexican or Indian background. Those people had little or no knowledge of Masonry. Their church discouraged Masonic affiliation. . . . Yet perhaps the greatest need of these men was friendship with those holding like beliefs."[102]

"There are many common themes and ideals in Masonic and Jewish rituals, symbols, and words. Judaism's most basic teaching is to believe in God who created everything in our existence and who gave us laws to follow, including the requirements to act honorably and kindly toward everyone. Belief in God, prayer, immortality of the soul, charity, and acting respectfully to all people are essential elements of Freemasonry as well as Judaism, and of course other religions too."[103]

According to the Institute for *Marrano-Anusim* Studies (Casa Shalom), crypto-Jews living in Spain have participated in masonic organizations. Their involvement in freemasonry might have been a form of networking for "advancement and integration" into the societies to which the *"Marranos"* migrated. [104]

### Menorah

"Candelabrum. There were seven branches in the original oil menorah used in the Tabernacle (Exo. 25:37) and later in Solomon's Temple. It is this menorah that Titus is said to have carried away after the destruction of the Temple and that is pictured in bas-relief on the Arch of Titus in Rome. On Hanukkah an eight-branched menorah (plus a shammash, or servant candle) is lit to commemorate the Maccabean victories."[105]

Cecil Roth, in his book, *The Religion of the Marranos*, explains: "The handful of twentieth-century references to crypto-Jewish celebration of *Hanukkah*—such as the report that it is sometimes celebrated in Portugal as the Feast of the Little Candles or even 'Little Christmas'—probably derive from the modern Jewish observance of *Hanukkah* or the calendar association of *Hanukkah* with Christmas" (qtd. in Gitlitz 377).[106]

### Messianism

"The belief that Jewish people and all humanity would be led to a golden age of perfect justice and universal peace by a Messiah, an ideal king and a perfect man. The Hebrew *mashiah* means 'one anointed with oil,' the ancient way of dedicating a man to a special service or office. *Mashiah Adonai,* the Anointed of God, was a title of honor given in the Bible to the kings of Israel."[107]

"A second set of crypto-Jewish beliefs dealt with the concept of the Messiah. Medieval Jews rejected the idea that Jesus was the Messiah or indeed that the Messiah had come."[108]

"Many *conversos* believed that the apocalyptic messianic age would not begin until the Jews had sufficiently atoned for their sins. . . . Of course many *conversos* thought that their most egregious sin was to have converted in the first place.

As Fernando de Madrid put it in 1491, before the Messiah could appear the *conversos* must first suffer for having become Christians."[109]

### Mezuza

"Why are *mezuzot* (singular, *mezuza*) placed on the doorposts of Jewish homes? The *mezuza* is a piece of parchment inscribed with verses from the Bible. It is rolled up, inserted in a case, and attached to the doorpost.

"That a *mezuza* be placed on the doorposts of every Jewish home is mandated in the Bible: 'And thou shalt write them [the commandments] upon the doorposts of thy house and upon thy gates' (Deuteronomy 6:9). Its function is twofold: to serve as a reminder of God's laws and to serve as a symbol of a Jew's loyalty to the Jewish people."[110]

"Why is the *mezuza* also called the *Shema*? The passage (Deuteronomy 6:4-9) written on the *mezuza* parchment begins with the word *shema*, 'hear.' The full verse is, 'Hear O Israel [*Shema Yisrael*], the Lord our God, the Lord is One' (Deuteronomy 6:4). Because of the popularity of this verse, which is part of every religious service and is also recited nightly as a bedtime prayer, many people refer to the *mezuza* by the first word of the verse."[111]

"Why is the *mezuza* kissed? It is Jewish tradition to kiss a holy object as a gesture of reverence. Many Jews follow the custom (of *Talmudic* origin) of touching the *mezuza* with the fingertips, kissing them, and reciting, 'May God protect my going out and coming in, now and forever.'"[112]

### Mis Christmas

Before Christmas, many *converso* children would go around to houses of grandparents, great-grandparents, etc. and receive small gifts. Father Clemente Carmona says, "I believe this is a leftover from *Chanukah*. I remember going to my grandparents and great-grandparents and receiving nuts, oranges, apples, and sometime coins wrapped in cloth."[113]

"During *Chanukah* it is customary to distribute coins . . . to the children.

"Reason: The Greeks wanted to tear the *Torah* from *Am Yisrael*. Accordingly it is necessary during these days to intensify honor for the *Torah* by encouraging the children to study. As the Rambam (Hil. Teshuvah 10:5) writes: 'Therefore when we teach the children . . . we initially teach them to serve *Hashem* out of fear, and then to receive reward.' And in his commentary on the *Mishnah* (to Sanhedrin ch. 10), the Rambam describes how the teacher induces the young student to learn *Torah*. 'The teacher says to him: Read [a little] and I will buy you pretty shoes, or precious clothes. Afterwards the *rebbe* should tell him: Learn this *parashah* or that chapter and I will give you a *dinar* or two.' For this reason during *Chanukah* we distribute prize money to the children so they should study *Torah* more."[114]

### Mitzvot

"In its strictest sense, it refers only to commandments instituted in the *Torah*; however, the word is commonly used in a more generic sense to include all of the laws, practices and customs of *halakhah*, and is often used in an even more loose way to refer to any good deed."[115]

See also **Halakhah**

### Names

"The northern half of Portugal . . . became an enclave of exiled openly practicing Spanish Jews and Crypto Jews pretending to be New Christians. Not surprisingly, new townships bearing identical names of older Spanish villages began to dot the landscape. At the same time, many families seemed to have dropped their actual last names and adopt the names of their family's hometown. Only when arrested by the Inquisition—and usually under torture or threat thereof—did the true family name emerge. Those never arrested—as well as those who 'could not remember' or 'did not know' the names of their relatives and ancestors—would forevermore carry the names of the provinces and/or townships from which their families had been expelled."[116]

Stephen Gilman, in his book, *The Spain of Fernando de Rojas,* explains: "At first *conversos* routinely took three sorts of surnames: the name of the town where they lived, or of the saint on whose day they were baptized or the church in which they were baptized, or of the Christian godparents who stood up with them at the baptismal font" (qtd. in Gitlitz 202).[117]

### Father Carmona

"Firstborn children were often given the same names from generation to generation. My grandfather was Clemente; my great-grandfather was Clemente; I am Clemente. If a Clemente died and had property, as long as a living Clemente existed, the property stayed in the family. The oldest had the same name down through the generations. It would perhaps confuse the Inquisition."[118]

### New Christians

"Riots took place in Toledo in 1449, but this time the victims were not the Jews. Now the *conversos* and their descendants, or *nuevos cristianos*, bore the brunt of the local anger; society was divided again, but this new division separated the Old Christians from the New Christians. The latter included those who had been baptized at birth as Christian and experienced their entire lives as Christians, but whose ancestors had converted some time earlier. A new basis of exclusion had been created: one's origin was now the essential factor. Following the violence there, the municipality of Toledo in 1449 established the *Sentencia-Estatuto*, excluding Jews and *conversos* of Jewish origin from public office; purity of blood (*limpieza de sangre*) was to become the essential requirement for one to hold civil or ecclesiastical office, to bear witness, to serve as a notary, or to display authority over an Old Christian."[119]

### New Moon

"*Rosh Hodesh* (New moon). Traditional Judaism considers each month's new moon a joyous occasion to be celebrated with special prayers. [Reneé Levine Melammed, in her book, *Women in (Post 1492) Spanish Crypto-Jewish Society: Conversos and the Perpetuation and Preservation of Observances Associated with Judaism*, explains:] The celebration does not appear to have been common among crypto-Jews, although there are very sporadic references such as those of Elvira de Mora [Alcázar, Castile 1590], who recalled observing the first day of the month as a holiday. . . . Genaro García, in his book, *Autos de fé de la Inquisición de México con extractos de sus causas, 1646-48*, explains:] The appearance of the new moon was observed festively in seventeenth-century Mexico. . . . Clara Núñez said her parents had taught her to 'worship the new moon, standing at the window, bowing to it the way her uncle did' " (qtd. in Gitlitz 393-94). [120]

### New Spain

"The Spanish throne divided its New World colonies into viceroyalties. The first two were Mexico and Peru, or, as they were known officially, New Spain and New Castile. . . . Mexico consisted of what is now the southwestern United States, all of Mexico and Central America, the Spanish islands in the Caribbean, principally Santo Domingo, Puerto Rico, Cuba, and, in the Far East, the Philippines."[121]

### Old Testament

"The name given to the Hebrew Bible [to] distinguish it from Christianity's New Testament." [122]

### Pan De Semita

"This unleavened bread still prepared and eaten by the descendants of the Crypto Jews and their Christian counterparts of northeast Mexico and South Texas during Lent, which happens to coincide with the Feast of Passover, can be found with or without raisins and/or pecans. . . . The *Autos de Fé* of 1646 through 1648, recorded the identities of the women who used to make the unleavened bread in Mexico City and Veracruz."[123]

"*Pan de Semita* was eaten in pre-inquisition Spain by a Jew or an Arab Moor. Today, it's popular in Texas and in that part of Mexico bordering Texas. It translates into English as 'Semitic Bread'. It's a Mexican-American custom in the Texas and Tex-Mex border area today to eat pan de semita during Lent which occurs on or around the Jewish Passover."[124]

### Panocha

One of the ingredients of capirotada is "the 'old world' sugar known as '*panocha*.'"[125]

See also **Capirotada**

### Passover

"[Following is one of] the religious beliefs of the Jews of the late sixteenth and most of the seventeenth century. . . . *Pacua de ceceño*, The Festival of Unleavened Bread, falls on March 14. (Actually, Passover never falls that early. There is no specific secular date because of the Jewish use of the lunar calendar for religious observances.) To deceive Christians, the word *Phase* was substituted for the name of Passover."[126]

"In Hebrew, *Pesach.* Anniversary of Israel's liberation from
Egyptian bondage. The holiday begins on the fourteenth day
of *Nisan* and lasts for eight days. It reminds each Jew that if
God had not freed his forefathers 'he and his sons and the
sons of his sons would still be slaves to Pharaoh in Egypt.'"[127]

"The *matzot,* or unleavened bread, which gives Passover
the name *Hag Hamatzot,* the Feast of Unleavened Bread, is
eaten in memory of the unleavened bread prepared by the
Israelites during their hasty flight from Egypt, when they had
no time to wait for the dough to rise. Since no leavened bread
or food containing leaven may be eaten during Passover,
special dishes and household utensils are used during the
eight-day observance. Laws are prescribed for the cleaning
or scalding in boiling water of utensils which are used
throughout the year but also on this holiday."[128]

"On this occasion, the *Haggadah,* or narration, is chanted
as the events of the Exodus from Egypt are told. . . . The
*Seder* service is one of the most colorful and joyous occasions
in Jewish life. It is adorned with ancient ceremonies and
symbols which recall the days when the Children of Israel
were liberated from Egypt."[129]

"The chanting of *Shir Hashirim* (*Song of Songs*) adds a
spring-like atmosphere at the end of the *Seder* service.
Symbolically, it is a song of love between God and the people
of Israel."[130]

"The *Talmud* lists five grains that may be used to make
*matza* for Passover. Joseph Caro, the Sephardic author of
the *Shulchan Aruch,* states that rice and other legumes (*kitnit*
or *kitniot* in Hebrew) may be used during Passover. Sephardic
Jews follow this ruling.

"The Ashkenazic community, following the lead of Moses
Isserles, prohibits the use of rice and legumes not because
Jewish law bans them directly, but because their use might
lead to possible confusion in the kitchen."[131]

"Eating cactus and egg omelets is a custom during the Passover week/Lent of secret Jews of the 17thcentury and of Mexican Americans from Texas and northern Mexico today. The omelets are called *nopalitos lampreados*. It's a custom to eat only this food during Lent."[132]

"The egg—A hard boiled egg represents the Holiday Offering in the days of the Holy Temple. The meat of this animal constituted the main part of the Passover meal." [133]

"Bitter herbs remind us of the bitterness of the slavery of our forefathers in Egypt. Fresh horseradish, romaine lettuce and endive are the most common choices."[134]

"*Quelite* is a wild bitter herb common to northern Mexico, Texas and the U.S. Southwest. A number of families interviewed in the Lower Rio Grande Valley of Texas add bits of *quelite* to their Easter Sunday dinner as a side vegetable."[135]

Seymour B. Liebman, in his book, *The Jews in New Spain*, informs us that, "Some colonial Mexicans fasted during the day for the whole week of Passover. . . . Fasting 'had become so ingrained that many thought that every holiday had to be accompanied by a fast' " (qtd. in Gitlitz 384).[136]

### *Penitentes*

According to Alberto López Pulido, who researched the Penitentes, his area of concentration was "on their core religious concept of doing penance through charity, prayer, and the good example. He explains that for the Penitentes, prayer is a form of action and acts of charity are tantamount to prayer—and that both provide good examples to the brotherhood and the community at large."[137]

José Cabezudo Astraín, in *Los conversos de Barbastro y el apellido 'Santángel',* explains: "Prior to the Expulsion many *conversos* who were comparatively well off thought it their duty to help their financially disadvantaged Jewish friends and relatives, and the Hebrew word for charity, *tzedakah*, frequently appears in trials covering events of this period" (qtd. in Gitlitz 589).[138]

### Purification

"According to Leviticus 12:2-8 a woman is 'unclean' for seven days after the birth of a son and fourteen days after the birth of a daughter. She is 'impure' for periods of forty or eighty days respectively. . . . There are examples [according to Ramón Santa María, in his book, *Ritos y costumbres de los hebreos españoles*,] from the late fifteenth and early eighteenth centuries of *conversa* women refraining from entering a church for forty days after giving birth." [139]

Amílcar Paulo, in his book, *Os judeus secretos em Portugal*, explains: "Remnants of after-childbirth purification ceremonies have surfaced in this century among the *cristãos novos* of the Trás-os-Montes region of Portugal. Even today some *conversas* in Beiras and Trás-os-Montes do not go to church for forty days following childbirth" (qtd. in Gitlitz 209).[140]

### Purim

"The Feast of Lots. This holiday falls on the 14th of *Adar*, commemorating a day on which Jews were saved from their oppressors. Read on the evening and morning of the holiday, The Book of Esther relates how Haman drew lots to determine when to put Jews of Persia to the sword. Fortunately, Haman's scheme was foiled by the faithful Mordecai and by Queen Esther.

"*Purim* is celebrated with great merriment after the fashion of the Persian Jews who made their victory over Haman an occasion 'for feasting and gladness.' During the reading of the Book of Esther, children twirl noisemakers in derision at every mention of Haman's name."[141]

"Among *conversos* much more popular than *Purim* itself was the Fast of Esther (*Ta'anit Esther*), which occurs on the thirteenth of *Adar*, the day before *Purim*, and commemorates the fact that Esther fasted before she approached King Ahasueros to plead for the Jews (Esther 4:15-16). Because fasts were much easier and safer for the crypto-Jews to keep than feasts, the Fast of Esther grew to rival the feast on the following day and eventually came to be the equal of the fast of *Yom Kippur*. . . . Later generations of new-Christians frequently referred to her as Saint Esther, a name by which she is recalled by remnant new-Christian communities in the twentieth century, among whom she is venerated almost like a Christian Saint."[142]

"[*Purim*] was not celebrated in the New World as the happy holiday known to other Jews. The crypto-Jews compared themselves to Esther, Mordecai, and the Jews who lived under the rule of the Medes and Persians and who were threatened with annihilation because of the machinations of *Haman*."[143]

### Quelite

"Apart from being the required bitter herb of the Passover *Seder* usually served with *cabrito* (instead of lamb), the Spanish colonial folk song of unknown authorship titled 'El Quelite' is of utmost interest."[144]

### Rosh Ha-shanah

"Literally, the New Year. The cycle of the High Holidays begins with *Rosh Ha-Sha*nah. Falling on the first and second days of the month of *Tishri*, it introduces the Ten Days of Penitence, when Jews examine their souls and take stock of their actions. The season, beginning with the New Year on the first day of *Tishri* and ending with *Yom Kippur*, the Day of Atonement, on the tenth, is known as 'Days of Awe.' The tradition is that on *Rosh Ha-Shanah* God sits in judgment on humanity. Then the fate of every living creature is inscribed in the Book of Life or Death. These decisions may be revoked by prayer and repentance before the sealing of the books on *Yom Kippur*." [145]



### *Sabbath*

"The climax of the Jewish week is the *Sabbath*, the seventh day of the week. The holiness of the *Sabbath* is stressed in the fourth commandment (Ex. 20:8-11), 'Remember the *Sabbath* Day to keep it holy. Six days shall you labor and do all thy work, but the seventh day is a *Sabbath* Day unto the Lord thy God.' "[146]

"It is an everlasting sign between God and Israel: 'For in six days the Lord made Heaven and Earth and on the seventh he ceased from work and rested' (Ex.31:17). The *Sabbath* day also is a reminder of the liberation from Egyptian bondage. It has served as a lesson to all humankind, proclaiming the need of human beings for a day free from labor and devoted to spiritual matters."[147]

"The *Sabbath* was observed from the setting of the sun on Friday until after sunset on Saturday [according to religious beliefs of the Jews of the late sixteenth and most of the seventeenth century]. Two people testified that one must see three stars in the heavens on Saturday night before the *Sabbath* was considered terminated. (This is still regarded as correct.) Clean shirts must be worn on the *Sabbath* 'similar to the custom of the Christians on Sunday.' The *Sabbath* is a reminder of the creation of the world and that God rested on the seventh day after completing His work. Therefore, during the *Sabbath*, no kind of work might be performed. Some shopkeepers opened their stores on the *Sabbath* to avoid suspicion of being a Jew, but they made no sales and accepted no money. Psalms of praise should be sung on the *Sabbath*, no fires should be lit, and only those foods prepared prior to the advent of the *Sabbath* might be eaten."[148]

### Saints

"In the seventeenth century, there was a common use of *Santo*, 'saint,' as a title for Moses and several Jewish prophets. This is an old Spanish custom and not the result of acculturation from Christianity, as were some other customs."[149]

### Salt

"Contamination being attributed in ancient and primitive thought to the machinations of demons, and salt being regarded as an incorruptible and cleansing substance, it was natural that the latter become a universally regarded potent against the evil forces. It was for this reason that mothers salted their babies, a ritual which included but was not limited to Hebrew women."[150]

"The common practice of bringing salt and bread into a new home before moving in, usually explained as symbolic of the hope that food may never be lacking there, was probably also in origin a means of securing the house against the spirits."[151]

### Sephardim

"Sephardim [are the] Jews of Spain and Portugal or their descendants, distinguished from the Ashkenazim chiefly by their liturgy, religious customs and pronunciation of Hebrew."[152]

### Shema

"The declaration of faith in the unity of God, traditionally recited mornings and evenings: 'Hear, O Israel, the Lord our God, the Lord is One' (Deut. 6:4-9)."[153]

"When Hebrew prayer books disappeared, only the most fundamental and frequently repeated Hebrew prayers remained in the communal consciousness: the affirmation of the oneness of God (the *Shema*); the daily blessings; and recurrent portions of daily, *Sabbath,* and festival prayers such as the *Kaddish*, the *Amidah*, and a number of blessings and hymns.  Those prayers which were not already firmly committed to memory disappeared almost instantly."[154]

"The central and most common precept for the Iberian crypto-Jews was the belief in a unitary God in contrast to what they considered to be the tripartite or plural God of the Christians.  Jews are uncompromising monotheists for whom belief in a single God is the most important article of faith.  The affirmation of monotheism is the first two of the Ten Commandments (Exodus 20:2-3) and the substance of Judaism's most often repeated prayer, the *Shema*."[155]

### Shivah

"This stage covers the seven days following burial and includes the three-day period of lamentation.  During this time, the mourner emerges from the stage of intense grief to a new state of mind in which he is prepared to talk about his loss and to accept comfort from friends and neighbors. . . .  *Sheloshim*-This period consists of the thirty days (counting the seven days of *shivah*) following burial.  The mourner is encouraged to leave the house after *shivah* and to slowly rejoin society. . . . The twelve-month period (counted from the day of burial) [is the time] during which things return to normal, and business once again becomes routine."[156]

See also **Yahrzeit**

### Siddur

"The daily prayer book.  Since prayer in a synagogue came to take the place of animal sacrifices after the destruction of the Second Temple, the prayers in the *Siddur* were arranged to follow closely the order of sacrifices in the Temple.  The three daily services are included in all daily prayer books, though some editions contain numerous additions, such as the Psalms and *The Song of Songs*. Many editions of the daily prayer books include the *Sabbath* and Festival prayers, as well as *Pirke Avot* (The Ethics of the Fathers). The oldest of the prayers is the *Shema* (Hear, O Israel)."[157]

### Superstition

"Superstitious beliefs and practices were common to all Jews, but some indulged in by the crypto-Jews were indigenous to the New World or to the villages in Spain or Portugal from which they or their parents had come."[158]

"Isolated on the outer edges of the Spanish North American Empire, far removed from the European Judaic centers of learning, *Talmudic* schools and *yeshivas*, orally passing down a set of religious beliefs, surrounded by hostile Indian cultures and constantly wary of being denounced by friend or foe to the Inquisition, many Sephardic practices and beliefs were easier to preserve and hand down as 'superstitious practices'. Those practices, however, vary from one family to another depending on (1) the degree of a family's assimilation to the Christian environment, (2) success of the concentrated 20th century Mexicanization effort, (3) impact of U.S. education, (4) residence distance from the U.S.-Mexico border, and (5) a family's socio-economic status."[159]

"Evil Eye. Superstition dating back to the *Talmud* and common among non-Jews as well, according to which someone may be cursed by someone else's evil glance. Amulets were used to ward off the evil eye." [160]

### Sweeping Away from the Door

"Many of the myths of the *marranos* concerned their mode of adapting domestic work to suit their lives; the most popular example was the way in which the judaizer was imagined to secretly clean the house for the *Sabbath*. Normally, after the house was swept, the front door was opened so the accumulated dirt could be swept outside. *Marranos* supposedly swept their dirt under the rugs so that no one (at least outside of the house) could witness the act. Again, it is housework that might expose the crypto-Jew to the outside world."[161]

### Tallit

According to Haim Beinart, in his book, *Records of the Trials of the Spanish Inquisition in Ciudad Real: 1483-1485*, "The *tallit*, or ceremonial pray shawl, is worn by orthodox Jewish men in prayer as a reminder of the obligation to comply with God's commandments in fulfillment of the prescription in Numbers 15:38-39, which states: 'bid them make tassels on the corners of their garments throughout their generations, and to put upon the tassel of each corner a cord of blue; and it shall be to you a tassel to look upon and remember all the commandments of the Lord.' Very often the shawls were woven with stripes of blue—or sometimes black—thread in compliance with the biblical requirement. The practice was common enough to be listed in the Inquisition's compilations of customs, such as a Valencian Edict of Grace of 1484, which labels as Judaizers people 'who instruct any Jew to wear the shawl, to venerate it and to kiss it in sign of devotion' " (qtd. in Gitlitz 524).[162]

According to Carlos Carrete Parrondo, in his book, *Proceso inquisitorial contra los Arias Dávila. Segovianos: un enfrentamiento social entre judíos*, "The prominent *converso* Diego Arias Dávila [Segovia 1460s] was variously described as 'praying with a sheet wrapped around his neck in the Jewish manner'; and 'with a linen taler on his head like a rabbi'; 'with a large shawl over his head and shoulders'; and 'wrapped in a tablecloth' " (qtd. in Gitlitz 524). [163]

Arturo Carlos de Barros Basto, in his book, *Tradicões Cripto-Judaicas*, explains: "The custom remains vital among some remnant crypto-Jews of this century. João Antonio Ferreira, at age 80 in 1929, talked about the crypto-Jewish community in Braganca. He said that 'on *Sabbaths* and fast days they put white linen towels on their heads when they said their prayers' " (qtd. in Gitlitz 525).[164]

## Talmud

"Literally, study or teaching. Legal code whose compilation spans almost 1,000 years. Based on the teachings of the Bible, the *Talmud* interprets biblical laws and commandments, branching out into many fields of knowledge. Although dealing primarily with law, the *Talmud* also contains a rich store of historic facts and traditions. In its pages are found scientific discussions, ethical teachings, legends, and profound observations on all phases of human experience."[165]

## Tanakh

"Though the word 'Bible' is commonly used by non-Jews—as are the terms 'Old Testament' and 'New Testament'—the appropriate term to use for the Hebrew scriptures ('scripture' is a synonym used by both Jews and non-Jews) is *Tanakh*."[166]

## Trinity

"The Christian belief in the Trinity—the Father, the Son, and the Holy Spirit has been viewed by Jewish scholars in two ways. To people such as Moses Maimonides (1135-1204), worship of a Trinity is polytheism; he called Christians 'heathens,' 'idolators,' violators of the commandment 'Thou shalt have no other gods before me' (Exodus 20:3). Maimonides, who was born in Spain but spent most of his life in countries where the dominant religion was Islam, considered only Jews and Muslims to be true monotheists."[167]

## Tu Bishevat

"Literally, the 15th day of Shevat, known as the 'New Year of Trees.' It marks the end of winter and the beginning of spring, and in ancient times people thought of it as the day in which sap begins to flow again in the trees. Before the Jews were driven from their land, it was celebrated with the festive planting of saplings. This custom has been revived in modern Israel."[168]

"In various places, the *Torah* compares a person to a tree: 'A person is like the tree of a field...' (Deut. 20:19) 'For as the days of a tree shall be the days of my people.' (Isaiah 65:22) 'He will be like a tree planted near water...' (Jeremiah 17:8). Why the comparison? A tree needs the four basic elements in order to survive—soil, water, air, and fire (sun). Human beings also require the same basic elements."[169]

When the Jews left Spain, many Sephardim took names from nature.

"It has been frequently stated that *conversos*, after being forced to abandon their Jewish names, chose surnames designating trees or others with a Catholic connotation, the latter to offer apparent proof of their loyalty to the new faith. . . . Mentioned as names of present-day descendants of crypto-Jews in the article by Eduardo Días are '*Pereira* (pear tree), *Carvalho* (oak tree).'"[170]

### *Yahrzeit*

"Observance of the anniversary of a death (*Yahrzeit*) began in *Talmudic* times. Death anniversaries of parents and teachers were observed as a sign of reverence for the deceased.

"The observance is old, but the word *Yahrzeit* was not used before the sixteenth century. Derived from the German *Jahrzeit*, it was used in the Christian Church to denote the occasion for honoring the memory of the dead."[171]

"Each year the anniversary of the death of a relative is

observed by lighting a special *yahrzeit* (anniversary) candle and reciting the *Kaddish*."[172]

Ramón Santa María explains: "A document from the late fifteenth century mentions *conversos* 'sitting on the floor behind closed doors where they eat fish, olives, but not meat, and out of grief for the deceased they do not leave the house for a year' " (qtd. in Gitlitz 296).[173]

"The three-day, month, and year-long periods were also observed sporadically well up into modern times. Modern remnant crypto-Jews conform to this pattern."[174]

See also **Shiva**

## Yarmulke

"A *yarmulke*, called a *kipa* in Hebrew, is a skullcap worn by Jews. Some wear one at all times, others only during prayer and at mealtime.

"The earliest Jewish reference to a head covering can be found in Exodus 28:4, where it is called a *mitznefet*. It was part of the wardrobe of the High Priest. In other biblical references, the covering of the head and face is regarded as a sign of mourning (II Samuel 15:30). The *Talmud*, however, associates the wearing of a headgear more with the concept of reverence (to God) and respect (for men of stature)."[175]

"The male custom of praying only when one's head is covered is not prescribed in the Bible, and in fact even into medieval times was an optional custom. But by the fifteenth century it had become a fairly widespread way of showing modesty before God."[176]

## Yom Kippur

"Literally, Day of Atonement. Regarded as the holiest day

**Gloria Golden**

in the year and known as the '*Sabbath* of *Sabbaths*,' *Shabbat Shabbaton.* A day of appeal for the forgiveness of sins, it is marked by fasting from sundown of the ninth to sunset of the tenth of *Tishri.*"[177]

"[This was a] religious [belief] of the Jews of the late sixteenth and most of the seventeenth century. . . . On the Great Day of Pardon (*Quipur*), God judged all humans. This day falls on the 10th day of September. (This is another incorrect date. When Manuel de Mello in Guadalajara wanted the community to observe *Quipur* on a date approximating the correct Hebrew date, a great fight ensued between his followers and those who insisted on using September 10. This date appears in Inquisition document 1254 in the Archivo Histórico Nacional de Madrid.) *Quipur* should be observed by fasting and praying for twenty-five hours. No one should sleep."[178]

# NOTES

1. Seymour B. Liebman, *New World Jewry, 1493-1825: Requiem for the Forgotten* (New York: KTAV Publishing House, Inc., 1982) 216.

2. Liebman, *New World Jewry* 31.

3. "Ashkenazim," *The Shengold Jewish Encylopedia*, 1998 ed. 34.

4. Seymour B. Liebman, "The Jews of Colonial Mexico," *The Hispanic American Historical Review* 43.1 (1963): 106.

5. Richard G. Santos, *Silent Heritage* (San Antonio: New Sepharad Press, 2000) 389.

6. David M. Gitlitz, *Secrecy and Deceit: The Religion of the Crypto-Jews* (Philadelphia: The Jewish Publication Society, 1996) 546.

7. Gitlitz, *Secrecy and Deceit* 546-47.

8. Liebman, *New World Jewry* 102.

9. Gitlitz, *Secrecy and Deceit* 548-49.

10. "Bar Mitzvah," *The Shengold Jewish Encyclopedia* 43.

11. Gitlitz, *Secrecy and Deceit* 223.

12. "Basque," *Webster's Encyclopedic Unabridged Dictionary of the English Language*, 1996 ed.

13. Myrna Katz Frommer and Harvey Frommer, "The Spanish-Jewish Connection: The Jews of the Basque," *Travel-watch.com* 2002, 2 Oct. 2002 http://www.travel-watch.com/Basque.htm .

14. Mechon-Mamre, "Prayers and Blessings," *Torah* 101, 11 Oct. 2002 http://www.mechon-mamre.org/jewfaq/prayer.htm .

15. Gitlitz, *Secrecy and Deceit* 443.

16. Gitlitz, *Secrecy and Deceit* 444.

17. Father Clemente Carmona, personal interview, 4 Jan. 2002.

18. Liebman, *New World Jewry* 163-64.

19. Gitlitz, *Secrecy and Deceit* 454-55.

20. Rabbi Isaac Klein, "Blessings Before Food," *Jewish Virtual Library* 1988, 27 Nov. 2002 http://www.us-israel.org/jsource/Judaism/blessfood.html .

21. Gitlitz, *Secrecy and Deceit* 452.

22. Mechon-Mamre, "Prayers and Blessings."

23. Gitlitz, *Secrecy and Deceit* 452.

24. Alfred J. Kolatch, *The Second Jewish Book of Why* (Middle Village: Jonathan David Publishers, Inc., 1985) 231.

25. David M. Gitlitz and Linda Kay Davidson, *A Drizzle of Honey* (New York: St. Martin's Griffin, 2000) 270.

26. Alfred J. Kolatch, *The Jewish Book of Why* (Middle Village: Jonathan David Publishers, Inc., 1981) 63.

27. Renee Levine Melammed, *Heretics or Daughters of Israel? The Crypto-Jewish Women of Castile* (New York: Oxford University Press, 1999) 89.

28. Liebman, *New World Jewry* 124.

29. Rabbi Amy B. Bigman, "Death and mourning: Jewish Rituals," *The Ecumenical Institute for Jewish–Christian Studies* Sept. 2000, 31 Jan. 2001 http://www.j-cinstitute.org/Articles/Bigman_Back_Jewish_Rituals.htm .

30. Melammed 89-90.

31. Liebman, *New World Jewry* 101.

32. Shmuel Pinchas Gelbard, *Rite and Reason: 1050 Jewish Customs and Their Sources* (Petach Tikvah, Israel: Mifal Rashi Publishing, 1995) 645-46.

33. Kolatch, *The Jewish Book of Why* 64.

34. Kolatch, *The Jewish Book of Why* 67.

35. Kolatch, *The Jewish Book of Why* 74.

36. Kolatch, *The Jewish Book of Why* 74.

37. Kolatch, *The Jewish Book of Why* 77.

38. Kolatch, *The Jewish Book of Why* 62.

39. Kolatch, *The Jewish Book of Why* 49.

40. Kolatch, *The Jewish Book of Why* 52.

41. Anne deSola Cardoza, "Texas Mexican Secret Spanish Jews Today," *Sefarad.org* 1997, 5 Nov. 2001 http://www.sefarad.org/publication/lm/011/texas.html .

42. Gitlitz, *Secrecy and Deceit* 56.

43. "Circumcision," *The Shengold Jewish Encyclopedia* 62.

44. Gitlitz, *Secrecy and Deceit* 205.

45. Melammed 17.

46. Eliezer Segal, "Columbus's Medinah?" *Calgary Jewish Free Press* 14 Oct. 1991, 5 Aug. 2003 elsegal@acs.ucalgary.ca .

47. "Bartolome De Las Casas (1484-1566)," Oregon State University, 11 Dec. 2002 http://www.orst.edu/instruct/ph1302/philosophers/las_casas.html .

48. "Las Casas, Bartholome de, 1474(?)-1566(?)" University of Chicago 2002, 5 Aug. 2003 http://www.alexanderstreet2.com/EENALive/bios/A6919BIO.html.

49. Benedict M. Ashley, "Reformers (1500s)," *The Dominicans* 1990, 5 Aug. 2003 http://www.op.org/domcentral/study/ashley/dominicans/ashdom05.htm .

# Crypto-Jews 259

50. Dr. Seth Ward, "Sephardim and Crypto-Judaism: Definition of Terms and Brief History." University of Denver, 27 Nov. 2003 http://www.du.edu/~sward/sephardim.html .

51. Kolatch, *The Second Jewish Book of Why* 53.

52. Kolatch, *The Second Jewish Book of Why* 53.

53. Kolatch, *The Second Jewish Book of Why* 53.

54. Gitlitz, *Secrecy and Deceit* 528.

55. Santos 388.

56. Liebman, *New World Jewry* 36.

57. Rebbe at LaMeD Academy of Malchi-Zedek, e-mail to the author, 21 March 2001.

58. María V, e-mail to the author, 2 Nov. 2003.

59. Temple Emanu El, "*Chanukah* Traditions," *info@TEECleve.org* 2003, 10 Dec. 2003 http://www.teecleve.org/hop/holiday/holiday-*Chanukah*_traditions.php .

60. "The Alhambra Decree," *The Nahman Home Page*, 17 Oct. 2002 http://home.earthlink.net/~bnahman/Alhambra_Decree_Abrabanels_Answer.htm .

61. "Education in Jewish History," *The Shengold Jewish Encyclopedia* 73-74.

62. "Education in Jewish History," *The Shengold Jewish Encyclopedia* 74.

63. "Education in Jewish History," *The Shengold Jewish Encyclopedia* 74.

64. "Education in Jewish History," *The Shengold Jewish Encyclopedia* 75.

65. Gitlitz and Davidson, *A Drizzle of Honey* 222-23.

66. Santos 346-47.

67. Gitlitz, *Secrecy and Deceit* 246.

68. Melissa Bromfman de Ferrante, "Crypto-Jews in Colonial Mexico," working paper, 2000, 11 June 2002 http://hemi.nyu.edu/archive/studentwork/colony/Ferrantepaper.htm .

69. Ferrante, "Crypto-Jews."

70. Mechon-Mamre, "Halakhah: Jewish Law," *Torah 101* 2003, 5 Aug. 2003 http://www.mechon-mamre.org/jewfaq/halakhah.htm .

71. Mechon-Mamre, "Halakhah."

72. "Hanukkah," *The Shengold Jewish Encyclopedia* 103.

73. Gitlitz, *Secrecy and Deceit* 376.

74. "Inquisition," *The Shengold Jewish Encyclopedia* 125.

75. Erna Paris, *The End of Days* (Amherst: Prometheus Books, 1995) 159.

76. Paris 166.

77. Gitlitz, *Secrecy and Deceit* 116.

78. C. Castelar, "Cattle, Cotton and Torah." *Sepharadchai* 1999, 23 Jan. 2003. http://www.geocities.com/Paris/LeftBank/1300/.

79. "Kaddish," *The Shengold Jewish Encyclopedia* 153.

80. Gitlitz, *Secrecy and Deceit* 288-89.

81. Kolatch, *The Jewish Book of Why* 85-86.

82. Kolatch, *The Jewish Book of Why* 88-89.

83. Liebman, *New World Jewry* 106.

84. Mechon Mamre, "Kashrut: Jewish Dietary Laws," *Torah 101*, 5 Aug. 2003 http://www.mechon-mamre.org/jewfaq/kashrut.htm .

85. Liebman, *New World Jewry* 119.

86. Gitlitz, *Secrecy and Deceit* 547.

87. Gitlitz, *Secrecy and Deceit* 545.

88. Gitlitz, *Secrecy and Deceit* 557.

89. Santos 355.

90. Richard Schwartz, Ph.D, "The Custom of *Kapparot* in the Jewish Tradition," http://www.jewishveg.com/schwartz, 13 Feb. 2002 http://schwartz.enviroweb.org/kapparot.html .

91. Mechon- Mamre, "Kashrut."

92. Ankica Petrovic and Mischa Livingstone, "The Key from Spain," *The National Center for Jewish Film*, 28 Jan. 2003 http://www.brandeis.edu/jewishfilm/keyfromspain.html .

93. María V., e-mail to author, 15 Dec. 2003 saudades-sefarad@yahoogroups.com .

94. Eduardo Mayone Dias, "Rituals and Practices Among the Secret Jews of Portugal," University of California, Los Angeles 1997, 6 April 2000 http://www.lusaweb.com/comunidades/rituals.html .

95. Gitlitz, *Secrecy and Deceit* 257.

96. Celiac Sprue Association, "Lactose Intolerance," ed. Mary Schluckebier, 17 Feb. 2002 http://www.csaceliacs.org/lactose.html .

97. Evergreen Nutritionals Online Store, "Lactase Enzyme," ed. Bill Spencer, 2 Aug. 2003 www.enutritionals.net .

98. "Ladino," *The Shengold Jewish Encyclopedia* 162.

99. "Magen David," *The Shengold Jewish Encyclopedia* 172.

100. Liebman, *New World Jewry* 36.

101. Liebman, *New World Jewry* 216.

102. Hon. Ray D. Carpenter, "Grand Lodge of New Mexico: Ancient Free & Accepted Masons," *nmmasons.org*, 14 March 2001 http://www.zianet.com/leon/gl.htm.

103. Paul M. Bessel, "Freemasonry & Judaism," 1998-2001, 17 Nov. 2003 http://www.bessel.org/masjud.htm.

104. Mrs. Gloria Mound, "Academic conference on the Jews and Freemasonry," *Casa Shalom* 2002, 30 Jan. 2003 http://www.casa-shalom.com/cs14.htm .

105. "Menorah," *The Shengold Jewish Encyclopedia* 179-80.

106. Gitlitz, Secrecy and Deceit 377.

107. "Messianism," *The Shengold Jewish Encyclopedia* 180.

108. Gitlitz, *Secrecy and Deceit* 103.

109. Gitlitz, *Secrecy and Deceit* 104.

110. Kolatch, *The Jewish Book of Why* 113.

111. Kolatch, *The Jewish Book of Why* 114.

112. Kolatch, *The Jewish Book of Why* 116.

113. Father Clemente Carmona, personal interview, 20 Nov. 2002.

114. Gelbard 449-50.

115. Mechon Mamre, "Halakhah."

116. Santos 6.

117. Gitlitz, *Secrecy and Deceit* 202.

118. Father Clemente Carmona, personal interview, 4 Jan. 2002.

119. Melammed 6.

120. Gitlitz, *Secrecy and Deceit* 393-94.

121. Liebman, *New World Jewry* 17.

122. "Old Testament," *The Shengold Jewish Encyclopedia* 199.

123. Santos 346.

124. Anne deSola Cardoza, "Texas Mexican Secret Spanish Jews Today."

125. Jim Carvalho, "Rios Grande," *Tucson Weekly* 7 Dec. 1999, 5 Feb. 2003 http://weeklywire.com/ww/12-07-99/tw_book.html.

126. Liebman, *New World Jewry* 106.

127. "Passover," *The Shengold Jewish Encyclopedia* 202.

128. "Passover," *The Shengold Jewish Encyclopedia* 202.

129. "Passover," *The Shengold Jewish Encyclopedia* 202.

130. "Passover," *The Shengold Jewish Encyclopedia* 203.

131. Kolatch, *The Second Jewish Book of Why* 334-35.

132. Anne deSola Cardoza, "Texas Mexican Secret Spanish Jews Today."

133. Lubavitch World Headquarters and your local Chabad-Lubavitch Center, "The Egg," ed. Chani Benjaminson 2000, 3 Oct. 2002 http://www.passover.net/passover/english/passoverTemplate.asp?Article ID=2000.

134. Lubavitch World Headquarters and your local Chabad Lubavitch Center, "The Bitter Herbs," ed. Chani Benjaminson 2001, 9 Oct. 2002 http://www.passover.net/passover/english/passover/Template.asp?ArticleID=2001.

135. Santos 349-50.

136. Gitlitz, *Secrecy and Deceit* 384.

137. Alberto López Pulido, *The Sacred World of the* Penitentes (Washington: Smithsonian Institution Press, 2000) back cover.

138. Gitlitz, *Secrecy and Deceit* 589.

139. Gitlitz, *Secrecy and Deceit* 209.

140. Gitlitz, *Secrecy and Deceit* 210.

141. *"Purim,"* *The Shengold Jewish Encyclopedia* 214.

142. Gitlitz, *Secrecy and Deceit* 378.

143. Liebman, *New World Jewry* 122.

144. Santos 350.

145. "Rosh Ha-Shanah," *The Shengold Jewish Encyclopedia* 220.

146. *"Sabbath,"* *The Shengold Jewish Encyclopedia* 226.

147. *"Sabbath,"* *The Shengold Jewish Encyclopedia* 226.

148. Liebman, *New World Jewry* 106-07.

149. Liebman, *New World Jewry* 101.

150. Charles Fensham (Ezekiel 16:4), "Salt As a Blessing and Curse in Ancient Times," *Jewish Heritage Online Magazine* 2002, 2 Feb. 2002 http://www.jhom.com/topics/salt/ancient.htm .

151. Joshua Trachtenberg, "Salting The Bread and The Baby: The Magical Powers of Salt," *Jewish Heritage Online Magazine* 2002, 2 Feb. 2002 http://www.jhom.com/topics/salt/magic.htm.

152. "Sephardim," *Webster's Encyclopedic Unabridged Dictionary of the English Language,* 1996 ed.

153. "Shema," *The Shengold Jewish Encyclopedia* 236.

154. Gitlitz, *Secrecy and Deceit* 40.

155. Gitlitz, *Secrecy and Deceit* 101.

156. Rabbi Maurice Lamm, "Jewish Way of Mourning," *Aish.com* 1995-2002, 6 June 2003 http://www.aish.com/literacy/lifecycle/The_Jewish_Way_of_Mourning.asp .

157. "Siddur," *The Shengold Jewish Encyclopedia* 238.

158. Liebman, *New World Jewry* 104.

159. Santos 354.

160. *"Evil Eye, "* *The Shengold Jewish Encyclopedia* 82.

161. Melammed 73. (See Simha Asaf, "The *Marranos* of Spain and Portugal in Responsa Literature" [Hebrew], Me'assef Zion 5 (1932-33):21, n.4. He claims that this "ancient custom" (in accusations made by Portuguese inquisitors), developed out of respect for the *mezuzah* on the doorpost.

162. Gitlitz, *Secrecy and Deceit* 524.

163. Gitlitz, *Secrecy and Deceit* 524.

164. Gitlitz, *Secrecy and Deceit* 525.

165. "Talmud," *The Shengold Jewish Encyclopedia* 255.

166. Jewish Virtual Library, "The Tanakh," *Shamash.org* 2002, 3 October 2002 http:// www.us-israel.org/jsource/Judaism/Tanakh.html .

167. Kolatch, *The Second Jewish Book of Why* 76.

168. "Tu Beshevat," *The Shengold Jewish Encyclopedia* 264.

169. Rabbi Shraga Simmons, "Man is a Tree," Aish.com 1995-2003, 7 March 2003  http://www.aish.com/tubshvat/tubshvatdefault/ Man_is_a_tree.asp.

170. Eduardo Mayone Dias, "Crypto-Jews in Portugal-A Clandestine Existence," *Jewish Virtual Library* 2000, 18 Dec. 2003  http://www.us-israel.org/jsource/vjw/Portugal.html.

171. Kolatch, *The Jewish Book of Why* 77-78.

172. "Yahrzeit," *The Shengold Jewish Encyclopedia* 56.

173. Gitlitz, *Secrecy and Deceit* 296.

174. Gitlitz, *Secrecy and Deceit* 296.

175. Kolatch, *The Jewish Book of Why* 121.

176. Gitlitz, Secr*ecy and Deceit* 527.

177. "Yom Kippur," *The Shengold Jewish. Encyclopedia* 288.

178. Liebman, *New World Jewry* 107

# SELECTED BIBLIOGRAPHY

This is a selected bibliography. The primary sources consulted for this work are indicated below.

Gitlitz, David. *Secrecy and Deceit: The Religion of the Crypto-Jews.* Philadelphia and Jerusalem: The Jewish Publication Society, 1996.

Kolatch, Alfred J. *The Jewish Book of Why.* Middle Village, NY: Jonathan David Publishers, Inc., 1981.

Kolatch, Alfred J. *The Second Jewish Book of Why.* Middle Village, NY: Jonathan David Publishers, Inc., 1985.

Liebman, Seymour B. *New World Jewry, 1493-1825: Requiem for the Forgotten.* New York: KTAV Publishing House, Inc., 1982.

Melammed, Renee Levine. *Heretics or Daughters of Esrael? The Crypto-Jewish Women of Castile.* New York: Oxford University Press, 1999.

Paris, Erna. *The End of Days.* Amherst, NY: Prometheus Books, 1995.

Santos, Richard. *Silent Heritage.* San Antonio: New Sepharad Press, 2000.

*The Shengold Jewish Encyclopedia.* Eds. Mordecai Schreiber, Alvin I. Schiff, Leon Klenicki. Rockville, MD: Schreiber Publishing, Inc., 1998 ed.

Printed in the United States
26415LVS00003B/1-51

9 780915 745562